Ask the Apostle

Faith-Building Conversations with Paul

N.D. Morrison

WalkWell Publishing

British Columbia, Canada

ASK THE APOSTLE

Faith-Building Conversations with Paul
by N.D. Morrison

Copyright © 2018 by N.D. Morrison

All rights reserved. No part of this book may by reproduced, transmitted, or stored in a retrieval system in any form or by any means without the written permission of the author or publisher, except for brief quotations within a book review.

Scripture verses have been adapted from the Open English Bible under terms of the CC0 license, and from the public domain World English Bible and New Heart English Bible.

Published by WalkWell Publishing, a ministry of Wholeness in Christ Ministries. Visit our website at www.wholenessinchrist.com, or contact WalkWell Publishing at PO Box 137, Saanichton BC V8M 2C3, Canada.

ISBN: 978-1-7751427-0-6 (print edition)

ISBN: 978-1-7751427-1-3 (e-book)

Printed in Canada

Cover photo by Penn Clark, Word of Grace Network
Editing by Janis Letchumanan, janisgrace.com
Book design by Jim Bisakowski, BookDesign.ca

    1 2 3 4 5 6   23 22 21 20 19 18

Contents

	Foreword	5
Chapter 1	Paul and His Gospel	7
Chapter 2	The World's Greatest Recall	21
Chapter 3	The Messiah Comes	35
Chapter 4	A New and Improved You	49
Chapter 5	Defeat Sin, Self, and Satan	64
Chapter 6	The Prize—Eternal Life	79
Chapter 7	God's Plan for You	93
Epilogue	Famous Last Words	107
	Ask the Apostle – Study Guide	117

*For all those who have
seen and tasted that the Lord
is good—and want more.*

*And for anyone else out
there who is wondering what
all the fuss is about.*

Foreword

We live in the age of smart assistants like Alexa, Siri, Bixby, and Cortana. Each provides us with knowledge and trivia at a moment's notice. With this book, Norm Morrison changes the paradigm and invites us to "Ask the Apostle" for truth about the great questions of the universe, including most importantly, the question of how we can live a full and vibrant life in a contrarian age.

Morrison draws the general reader and the scholar alike into the profound, multifaceted teaching of the apostle Paul through a series of imaginary dialogues and engaging narratives. Each is filled with keen insight and passion, which Morrison intersperses with humor and wit. The result is a text that draws the reader into a personal reflection of the real problem facing humans—namely, our need for a heart-mind transformation, not just a reformation.

The extensive, carefully prepared study notes make the book an ideal resource for group study. Taken together, the dialogue, the narrative, and the study guide present a culturally relevant and trustworthy synthesis of the answers God gave to one of the world's most influential individuals two thousand years ago. It is a synthesis that is timely, relevant, highly readable, and inspiring for today.

Dr. George Durance, TeachBeyond President
and Ambrose University, President Emeritus

1
Paul and His Gospel

More faith! More power! More of Jesus!

Time after time, over a span of two decades in ministry, these are the cries I heard from Christians in their homes, in coffee shops, and in the church. This book is my response to all those appeals for a more vibrant and fulfilling Christian life and walk.

When people become believers in Jesus Christ, they enter into a whole new realm of life—a spiritual realm. At first, they do not understand their new spiritual life, especially its power and the divine laws that govern it. But the apostle Paul fully understood this spiritual realm and how it works, and he spent years sharing his knowledge and experience with others. He travelled widely, proclaiming the good news and converting many people to this new life, and then he returned to disciple them and strengthen their faith.

These gatherings would have witnessed a lively exchange of questions and answers as new believers explored the deep truths of their salvation with the apostle. Paul then followed up these meetings with letters written to the congregations of Christians, repeating and reinforcing his conversations with them.

We have a record of Paul's letters in our Bible, making up nearly one-third of the New Testament. Many of them include his responses to specific questions and challenges the groups of believers were experiencing. Woven throughout these letters are also the inspired insights and teachings Paul had previously shared with them—written reminders to help them mature in their Christian faith and walk.

Today, when you open your Bible and read Paul's letters, have you ever thought, "Wouldn't it be great to talk to Paul directly? And to ask him questions, just like those early Christians did?"

Now, in a sense, you can! In this book, I simulate that experience by discussing the gospel and faith with Paul—asking him questions you might ask and possibly a few you haven't thought of yet. Paul's answers to my questions are derived from his letters as recorded in the Bible. His answers echo what he might have said in his meetings long ago with the very first Christians.

I imagined meeting Paul at his rented house in Rome where the Bible says he spent two years teaching about Jesus Christ and the kingdom of God. By this time Paul had completed several mission trips, had written letters to the new Christians, and was approaching the end of his life.

The Bible tells us Paul welcomed all who came to him, both Jews and Gentiles, so it was easy to envision him welcoming me. I could see Paul graciously inviting me into the cool of his stone house. I saw a few other people there as well, scattered around the room, chatting quietly with the shared confidence of regulars.

Paul and I sat on plain wooden chairs with a small table between us. I set my Bible on the table, explaining to Paul that it was a modern-day form of his parchments. I thought I knew my Bible pretty well, and I hoped to share some of that knowledge with others as we talked. As it turned out, I had a few things to learn myself.

Paul and the Law

I started by asking Paul about his background, his early ministry, and how he came by the gospel he preached so powerfully. I smiled and said, "Can we talk about you for a bit, Paul? You said you're a Jew."

"I am indeed a Jew."

"Born a Jew?"

"An Israelite by birth—of the tribe of Benjamin." Paul raised his chin ever so slightly. "Circumcised on the eighth day, I am a Hebrew of Hebrews." *Romans 11:1*

"Yes, well," I said, "that sounds pretty Jewish!"

"And as to the law, I am a Pharisee and as zealous in God's service as any other Jew." *Philippians 3:5*

I pointed to my Bible. "The Bible says you were taught by Gamaliel, a highly respected expert in Jewish law." *Acts 5:34*

"Indeed, I was brought up at his feet and taught in accordance with the strict system of our ancestral law." *Acts 22:3*

"The law God gave Moses," I said, nodding. "Plus all the extras." *Exodus 31:18*

"And all the Jews know and have always known," Paul said, "that in accordance with the very strictest form of our laws, I lived as a true Pharisee." *Acts 26:4–5*

"Paul, I thought a Pharisee is a Pharisee—you know, devoted to obeying the law." I narrowed my eyes. "What's a true Pharisee?"

"Just this," said Paul. "I was so zealous for the laws and traditions of my ancestors that I advanced well beyond many of my fellow Jews." *Galatians 1:14*

"Sounds like a race."

"And as to the righteousness based on those laws, I had proven myself blameless." *Philippians 3:6*

"A race to righteousness," I said. "And the finish line is heaven. You thought you could be made acceptable to God by obeying the law."

"It is our Jewish heritage." Paul looked at me and shrugged. "But all those things I once held as advantages, I now count as useless." *Philippians 3:7*

"That'd be a pretty strict life. What possible advantages—"

"What advantages has a Jew?" Paul's eyes widened. "Many—in every way!" He took a quick breath. "To start with, all the prophecies of God were entrusted to Jews. And, as Israelites, theirs was the adoption as sons. They were given the glory, the covenants, the promises, the—" *Romans 3:1–2; 9:4*

"Whoa, Paul! You threw all that away?"

Paul and His Gospel

"And more. The sign of circumcision. My zeal for the law. My own righteousness..." Paul dismissed it all with a wave of his hand. "I count it all as loss for the supreme good of knowing Jesus Christ."

"That certainly gives all-for-Jesus a whole new meaning."

"For Christ's sake I lost all these." Paul leaned in close to me. "I consider it all as dung."

"Strong words."

Philippians 3:8–9

"I gave it up to gain Christ," Paul said, settling back into his chair. "Not striving after my own righteousness from the law, but receiving a righteousness from God through faith in Christ."

"You sound more sold out for Jesus than you were for the law."

Galatians 3:21

"Listen! If a law had been given that could impart life, then righteousness would have been attained through the law."

"Paul, if anybody would know that"—I pointed at him with both hands and made a sharp click with my tongue—"it'd be you."

Romans 3:20

"As it is," Paul said, "nobody will be declared righteous in God's sight by obedience to the law."

"So if the law couldn't make people right with God," I said, "why have it?"

Galatians 3:19

"Because of sin," Paul said. "Until the coming of the promised one. It reveals sin for what it is."

"The promised one," I said. "Sounds like somebody had a plan."

Galatians 3:24

"The law was our tutor to lead us to Christ," Paul said, "that we may be pronounced righteous as the result of faith."

"And that's the gospel, isn't it?" Now I was leaning into Paul's space. "God in Christ reconciling the world to himself. Not counting our sins against us."

2 Corinthians 5:19

"Yes. The message of reconciliation." Paul looked at me and added, with a slight smile, "Which God entrusted to me."

"For you then, Paul, first it was the law and Judaism and then it was Jesus and—"

"The church," Paul said. "The church of the living God." He planted both hands firmly on the table. "It is the pillar and foundation of the truth." *1 Timothy 3:15*

"Well, we know you didn't always feel that way. In fact, you ravaged the church, bursting into homes and dragging men and women off to prison." *Acts 8:3*

Paul's head dropped. "Then you heard of my conduct when I was devoted to Judaism. How I persecuted the church of God, trying to destroy it." *Galatians 1:13*

"Whatever compelled you to do that?"

"My zeal for the law," Paul said. "As a Pharisee I believed it was my duty to oppose the name of Jesus of Nazareth." *Philippians 3:6; Acts 26:9*

"You were blinded by your faith in the law."

"I had authority from the chief priests," Paul said, "to throw many of Christ's followers into prison."

"Paul, you were filled with blind zeal!"

"And when it was proposed to put them to death, I voted against them." *Acts 26:10*

"They were killed for their faith in Jesus?"

"Putting men and women alike into chains and throwing them into prison, I persecuted them even to their death." *Acts 22:4*

"Oh Paul!"

"And I took vengeance on them in all the synagogues, punishing them to make them curse Jesus."

"How could you do these things?"

"I was zealous for God!" Paul threw up his hands. "Mad with rage against them, I even pursued them to foreign cities to hunt them down." *Acts 22:3; 26:11*

"What about the Ten Commandments?" I said. "Wasn't 'Do not kill' part of your law?" *Exodus 20:13*

"I had letters from the high priest himself and the council to take to synagogues in Damascus!" Paul closed his fist and *Acts 9:2; 22:5* clenched it so tight it trembled. "Authority to find Christ's followers and bring them to Jerusalem in chains to be punished."

Paul Meets Jesus

"Paul, let's just, ah…" I ran my hand over my face. "So you went from being one of the greatest enemies of the church to being one of its biggest allies. How come?"

"I met Jesus."

"You met Jesus," I said. Some of the people listening to us moved in closer. "Well, there's nothing like a personal testimony. Want to share some of it?"

"I was telling you," Paul said. "I was going to Damascus to find followers of Christ."

Acts 9:1

"Yes, and breathing threats and slaughter against them, I'm sure."

Paul lowered his eyes. "But I did it in ignorance." Then he lowered his head and mumbled something.

"Pardon me?"

1 Timothy 1:13

"I did it as an unbeliever," Paul said, looking up. "Though I used to blaspheme and persecute"—he slowly shook his head—"mercy was shown me because I did it in ignorance."

Luke 23:34

I pitied Paul in that moment…and thought of Jesus. "When they were crucifying Jesus, he asked God to forgive them because they didn't know what they were doing."

1 Timothy 1:15

"It is true," Paul said, "that Jesus Christ came into the world to save sinners." He looked around the room. "And there is no greater sinner than I."

"So there is hope for us all." I followed Paul's eyes around the room and nodded to a couple of people who seemed doubtful. "But back to your story."

Acts 22:6; 26:13

"Yes…Damascus," said Paul. "As I approached the city, at about noon, a light from heaven shone all around me. It was brighter than the sun."

"Yikes!"

"I fell to the ground! And I heard a voice saying, 'Saul, Saul, why are you persecuting me?'" — Acts 22:7

"We call you Paul."

"It was Saul…back then." — Acts 13:9

"OK, we have a blinding light, you falling, and a voice calling your name. What'd you do?"

"I was lying there trembling and dazed. I said, 'Who are you, Lord?' And he said, 'I am Jesus whom you are persecuting.'" — Acts 9:6; 22:8

"Quite a wake-up call."

"He told me to get up and stand on my feet. Then he said, 'I have appeared to appoint you as my servant and a witness of all that I shall reveal to you.'" — Acts 26:16

"Paul, this is incredible! The risen Jesus right there—talking to you."

"Because of the glory of the light I was unable to see." Paul squinted. He seemed to be reliving it. — Acts 22:11

"Take your time," I said. "We want to hear every detail."

"Jesus said he was sending me to others, to open their eyes and turn them from darkness to light—"

"Well, *you* sure saw the light!"

"—and turn them from the power of Satan to God, so they could receive pardon for their sins." Paul looked straight at me, his eyes burning into mine. "And inherit eternal life through faith in him." — Acts 26:17–18

"That's a big assignment," I said. "Where on earth do you start something like that?"

"The Lord told me to go into Damascus," Paul said, "and there I would be told all that I was appointed to do." — Acts 22:10

"You said you were blinded by the light."

"Those who were with me led me by the hand into the city. And there a man named Ananias came to see me."

"Who was Ananias?"

Paul and His Gospel

Acts 22:12	"He was a godly man according to our law. Respected by all the Jews there."

"Then Ananias was a Jew," I said.

Acts 22:13	"He said 'Saul, receive your sight.' And at that very hour I could see again."

"He was a Jew with healing powers."

Acts 22:16	"And then Ananias said, 'Why are you waiting? Get up and be baptized. Wash away your sins, calling on the name of the Lord.'"

"So he was a Jew who knew Jesus!" I said. "Is that where you got your gospel message?"

Galatians 1:12	Paul looked up sharply. "I did not receive it from man." He leveled a finger at me. "Nor was I taught it by man."

"Paul, I wasn't trying to—"

2 Corinthians 12:1–2, 4	"It was by direct revelation from Jesus Christ." Paul let out a breath—or perhaps a sigh. "Caught up to the third heaven…into Paradise itself. I could go on to visions and revelations from the Lord. Hearing inexpressible words which no man may tell."

"I didn't mean—"

2 Corinthians 12:5 Galatians 1:15–16	"And yet I will not boast of myself." Paul straightened up. "But when God revealed his Son in me that I might proclaim him to the Gentiles"—he wagged a finger at me—"I did not rush to consult with flesh and blood."

"Ah, yes, the Gentiles." I tried to change the subject. "All the non-Jews. People like me."

Galatians 1:17	"Nor did I go to Jerusalem to see those who were apostles before me," Paul said. "Instead I went into Arabia…and then back to Damascus."

"Preaching the gospel?"

Galatians 1:18–19	"For three years. Then I went up to Jerusalem to see Peter. I stayed with him 15 days." Paul nodded and thought for a moment. "I saw James too, the Lord's brother. But none of the other apostles."

Paul paused again, and I watched as a memory grabbed hold of him.

"It was many years later," Paul continued, "that I went up to Jerusalem again with Barnabas, taking Titus with me." *Galatians 2:1*

"Your partners in the gospel. Why Jerusalem?"

"I wanted to speak privately to the leaders there for fear that somehow I was running in vain," Paul said. "And I laid before the apostles the gospel I preached among the Gentiles." *Galatians 2:2*

"You wanted them to approve what you were teaching?"

Paul bristled. "It was all because of some false brothers who slipped in to spy on our freedom in Jesus Christ."

"Aha," I said. "It was that circumcision business, wasn't it? The Jewish sign of their covenant with God."

Paul groaned and shook his head. "They wanted to bring us back into bondage." *Galatians 2:4*

"The Jews received the new way of the gospel," I said, "but they couldn't let go of the old way to approach God."

"If you try to be pronounced righteous by the law, you have cut yourself off from Christ." Paul shuddered. "You have rejected the way of grace." *Galatians 5:4*

"They wanted to bring you back to their law," I said. "Circumcise the Gentile believers." I sucked air in through my teeth. "You didn't yield to them?"

"Not even for an hour," Paul said, "so the truth of the gospel would be preserved." *Galatians 2:5*

"Our freedom from the law."

"Indeed," said Paul, "for circumcision is of value only if you continue to do the works of the law." *Romans 2:25*

"You can't get right with God by cutting off some flesh."

"Beware of those dogs!" Paul's hand sliced across the table. "Those men who mutilate the flesh!" *Philippians 3:2*

I wanted to get us back to Paul's story. "So you knew you were right," I said. "You just wanted to check in with the leaders in Jerusalem."

"I did. And not even Titus was compelled to be circumcised." Paul smiled. "Even though he was a Greek."

<small>Galatians 2:3</small>

I winced. "Lucky for Titus."

"And I say again that every man who accepts circumcision must keep the law—all of it."

<small>Galatians 5:3</small>

"Lucky on a couple of levels."

"But even those men who are circumcised do not themselves keep the law," said Paul. "They do it only to avoid being persecuted for the cross of Jesus Christ."

<small>Galatians 6:12–13</small>

"And thus they cancel out their faith."

"For we are the true circumcision," Paul said. "We who worship God in the Spirit and rejoice in Jesus Christ."

<small>Philippians 3:3</small>

"This is great!" I clapped my hands and leaned toward Paul. "But we keep getting off your story. So who did you meet with in Jerusalem?"

"Those who were considered leaders. James, Peter, John—all acknowledged as pillars." Paul shrugged. "They added nothing to me."

<small>Galatians 2:6</small>

"Disciples of Jesus and his own brother," I said. "Leaders indeed! And they didn't tell you to change your message?"

"On the contrary," Paul said. "They saw that I had been entrusted with the gospel for the Gentiles, and they gave Barnabas and me the right hand of fellowship."

<small>Galatians 2:7, 9</small>

"Well, thanks be to God on behalf of all us Gentiles!" I grinned at Paul.

Paul's Gospel Ministry

"So this is what I'm hearing," I said. "You were jailing and killing the Jews who followed Jesus. You were going to Damascus to seize more of them when Jesus appeared to you and appointed you as his own personal witness." I spread my arms out. "What's that tell us?"

"God is abounding in mercy," Paul said.

"Abounding indeed," I said. "It tells me anybody can be saved."

I noted a few people around us nodding solemnly.

"And much more than mercy for you, Paul," I said. "Jesus appeared to his own disciples after he rose from the dead, and he appointed them as his witnesses." I touched Paul's shoulder. "He gave you that same honor."

"Though I saw him last of all." Paul looked away. "I am the least of them and not even worthy to be called an apostle, for I persecuted the church of God." Paul looked back to me. "But by the grace of God I am what I am."

"An apostle of Christ appointed to proclaim the gospel!" I said.

"And his grace toward me was not in vain," Paul said. "I worked harder than any of them. Journeys and perils in the wilderness, in the city, at sea. In hunger and thirst, in cold and nakedness." Paul sat motionless. "Jailed. Whipped. Beaten. Stoned…and left for dead."

"Definitely not your typical speaking tour."

"And always we labor," Paul said, "toiling with our own hands. I have never coveted anyone's gold or silver or clothing." Paul turned his palms up and looked at them. "These hands provided for my own needs and for my companions also."

I looked down at Paul's hands. Scarred. Strong. The hands of a tentmaker.

"Yet it was not I." Paul's eyes met mine. "It was the grace of God with me."

I looked down again. They were an apostle's hands.

"Paul, you began to proclaim the gospel right after your baptism—there in Damascus."

"But I have nothing to boast about, spreading the good news, for I am compelled to do it." Paul pursed his lips. "Woe to me if I do not proclaim the gospel."

"Even at the risk of death, it would seem. You spoke openly about Jesus Christ, insisting he is the Son of God." I pointed a

Ephesians 2:4

Acts 1:8

1 Corinthians 15:8–10

Romans 1:1

1 Corinthians 15:10
2 Corinthians 11:23–27

1 Corinthians 4:12
Acts 20:33–34

Acts 18:3

1 Corinthians 15:10

Acts 9:20

1 Corinthians 9:16

Acts 9:20
Matthew 27:23

cautionary finger at Paul. "That was pretty gutsy. The Jews had Jesus crucified for saying that."

Romans 1:1, 3–4

"But I was called for that very purpose! To tell God's good news about his Son, Jesus Christ." Paul's face lit up. "Descended from King David, yes, but revealed as the Son of God by his resurrection from the dead!"

"And how did the Jews take that little announcement?"

"They tried to kill me."

I couldn't help but smile. How the tables had turned.

Acts 9:22–24

"I stumped the Jews in the synagogues in Damascus," Paul said, "proving from Scripture that Jesus is the Messiah. So they plotted against me to kill me—watching at the city gates night and day."

"Tough spot to be in," I said. "You know the truth, but if you say it, they'll kill you."

Acts 9:25

"But I learned of their plot," Paul said, "and during the night the disciples let me down through the city wall in a basket."

"And off you went to proclaim the gospel—trying to keep ahead of those who wanted you dead or in jail." I caught Paul's eye. "Hounding and harassing you, just as you once did to the followers of Jesus."

Galatians 1:22–23

"Yes. Though I was still unknown by sight to the churches. They were only hearing that the same man who persecuted them was now preaching the very faith he tried to destroy."

"Sounds like you ended your old way of life in a bloodbath of persecution," I said. "And you began your new life in a bloodbath of another kind."

Ephesians 2:13

Paul thought for a moment, and as his eyes teared up, he said, "Brought near by the blood of Christ."

Revelation 1:5

"Jesus loved you," I said, "and washed away your terrible sins with his own blood."

"And it is now the love of Christ that compels me," Paul said.

"His love for you or your love for him?"

"Both," Paul said. "But his love for me. For us." He waved his hand across the room. "For all of us."

"Why do you say that?"

"Because I am convinced he died for all." Paul waved his hand again. "Therefore all died." — *2 Corinthians 5:14*

I made a mental note to unpack that one later.

"And he died for all," Paul said, "so the living should no longer live for themselves, but for him who died and rose for them." — *2 Corinthians 5:15*

"So now, for you, it's all about Jesus," I said.

"My whole life is for Jesus," Paul said. "For it is not me I proclaim, but the Lord Jesus Christ, and me a servant for his sake." — *2 Corinthians 4:5, 11*

"May we all be transformed like that."

"Like that and more." Paul beamed. "For one day Christ will transform our lowly body to be like his glorious body." — *Philippians 3:21*

"As I said, it sounds like someone has a plan. So I'll get right to it." I looked Paul square in the eyes. "We need your kind of faith—"

"That's my one desire," Paul said. "That we all come to the unity of the faith." — *Ephesians 4:13*

I looked around the room. "—and your power."

"The power is of God, not of us. We hold this treasure in frail human bodies." Paul ran his hand down his chest. "Clay pots." — *2 Corinthians 4:7*

"And that's why people need—oh, how to say this?" I fanned the pages of my Bible. "Faith, power—a godly life…for many it remains a mystery."

"Great indeed is the mystery of godliness," Paul said. "But there is a truth that produces a godly life." — *1 Timothy 3:16 / Titus 1:1*

"Will you teach us that? How to live a life that pleases God?"

Paul looked down, then shifted his gaze to the people around us. "I was appointed a preacher and an apostle." He slowly turned back to look at me.

"Preaching is good," I said, "but we need to be taught." I steeled myself for a "No."

"And I was also appointed"—I caught the hint of a smile—"a teacher." — *2 Timothy 1:11*

1 Corinthians 10:33

"I'll take that as a yes! Thank you, Paul—thank you!"

"Just as I try to please everybody in everything," Paul said, "not seeking my own gain, but for others, that they may be saved."

"Then let's get started!"

Paul looked eager, but he also looked tired. "In the morning," I added. "In the morning."

2
The World's Greatest Recall

Paul said he would help us understand the mystery of godliness—but where to start that conversation? There is so much to talk about, and our needs are so different. And yet, we are all the same in one respect: we are all born with a flaw, a defect. If I could just…and then it hit me!

Every year, many thousands of cars and trucks come off the assembly line with defects in them, ranging from fire and airbag hazards to faulty brakes and steering glitches. As a result, these vehicles don't always do the things they're supposed to do. And they sometimes do things they're not supposed to do. So the automakers recall the defective vehicles to fix them—free. Over the years, manufacturers have recalled millions of cars and trucks.

But there's another 'recall' out there today that is much, much bigger. You won't read about this recall in the newspapers, see it on TV, or catch it on the Internet. And yet it's there, and it affects more than seven billion people worldwide. That's because it is a recall on—people.

We have a defect. Just like those cars and trucks that get recalled for repairs, we don't work right. We don't always do the things we're supposed to do. And we often do the things we're not supposed to do.

We hate when we should love.

We take when we should give.

We lie when we should tell the truth.

We curse when we should bless.

We judge when we should forgive.

We get annoyed or angry when we should be patient or longsuffering. We're self-seeking, envious, and jealous of others. We're boastful and proud. We hold grudges. We cheat others, steal from them, and sometimes we even kill them. Newspapers and newscasts confirm this truth every day. Every hour.

We are born with an impulse within us to do wrong things. Bad things. Things we don't even like. And here's the kicker: we can't fix it. We have tried education, discipline, and yes, religion too. We've tried all that and more. We can't charm, beat, or starve it out of a person. We can no more fix ourselves than a defective car or truck can fix itself.

Now, we may not see or feel a defect in our car or truck right away. Often we won't even know about it until the manufacturer notifies us. There is an old saying, "What you don't know can't hurt you." But the fact is what you don't know *can* hurt you. Sudden acceleration. Loss of steering. Brake failure. Exploding gas tank. Ouch! So, when we hear about a defect in our vehicle, we want to get it fixed.

It's much the same with people. God, our creator, has identified a deadly defect in us. And he has issued a worldwide recall offering to fix it—free. We can go on with our life disbelieving the warning, ignoring it, or even making fun of it. But the fact remains: if we do have a serious defect and God has a fix for it, there is no need for us to drive off a bridge in the middle of the night because our brakes failed to stop us. Unless, of course, we didn't 'get' the recall notice.

I decided to start there with Paul.

The Fatal Defect

"Paul, I think people can go through their entire life not knowing that something is wrong with them."

Paul nodded as he pulled his chair closer.

"Personally," I said, "I went a long time thinking I was just fine. I believe it was that ignorance-is-bliss thing."

"That's right," Paul said. "And God overlooked the times of people's ignorance. But now he is announcing to everyone that they need to repent." *Acts 17:30*

"Actually, I'm thinking more in terms of recall than repent."

Paul looked puzzled.

"Recall," I said. "On account of their defect." I scratched my head. How do I explain a recall to someone who would think General Motors is an army officer and Ford is something you do to a river?

Paul started to fidget with his chair.

"It's like God is calling people back to him to get fixed," I said. "Same as repent, but that word isn't very popular anymore."

"It never was." Paul finally got his chair where he wanted it.

I scanned the room. As usual, people had gathered to listen—sitting on benches, the floor, one on a window ledge. Some new faces today.

"You were going to teach us how to have your kind of faith and power," I said.

"It is the wisdom of God that we teach," Paul said. *1 Corinthians 2:7*

"Exactly what we need to know."

"Things that eyes have never seen," Paul said. "Nor ears ever heard. Things that have never entered the heart of man."

"Yes—yes! What kind of things?"

"Things God has prepared for all those who love him." *1 Corinthians 2:9*

"We love God," I said. "Or at least we want to."

"Then do not reject his abundant mercy and patience," Paul said.

"But we don't." I looked around the room. "Well, maybe some of us do."

<small>Romans 2:4</small>

"Do you not know that his kindness is meant to lead you to repentance?"

"Exactly," I said. "God loves us and is calling us back to him to fix our defect. But I think it starts with our seeing that we're broken. That we don't work quite the way we should." I turned to look at Paul. "Don't you think?"

<small>Romans 3:9
Galatians 2:15</small>

"I have already said that Jews and Gentiles alike are all enslaved to sin."

<small>1 Corinthians 15:34</small>

Paul turned in his chair to address the room. "Some of you have no knowledge of God," he said, raising his voice. "Come to your senses, I say." As Paul turned back toward me, he added, "And stop sinning!"

I tried to redirect. "I think we should identify the defect," I said. "Give it a name."

"Sin."

"Excuse me?"

<small>Romans 14:23</small>

"Sin," Paul said. "For everything that is not from faith is sin."

"I'm trying to be subtle here," I said. "You know...defect, recall."

<small>Romans 3:22–23</small>

"There is no difference," Paul said. "For every person in the world has sinned."

"Yeah, it's just that every time I talk about that, people get all—"

<small>Romans 3:12</small>

"They have all gone astray," Paul said. "They have all become useless."

"I said something like that once, and a big guy poked his finger in my chest and said, 'That's my mother you're talking about.' So I just...stopped talking like that."

Paul cocked his head.

I motioned with my arms. "Very big guy."

"But Scripture says there is no one righteous," Paul said. "Not even one." — *Romans 3:10*

"Well, this guy sure didn't like to hear that." I winced at the recollection. "What would you have said to him?"

Paul thought for about half a second and said, "People deceive with their tongues. Their throats are like open graves. The venom of serpents lies behind their lips. Their mouths are full of bitter curses. Their feet race to shed blood. Distress and trouble dog their steps, and the way of peace they do not know." — *Romans 3:13–17*

"OK…" I slowly nodded my head. "Wish you could've been there." I looked at Paul. "But do you suppose his mom was really that bad?"

"The sins of some are plain to all," Paul said, "going before them to judgment. While the sins of others will appear later." — *1 Timothy 5:24*

"I did a survey once," I said. "Nine out of ten people believed we are born good. One couldn't decide."

"There is not one who does good." Paul shook his head. "No—not one."

"But people say we're basically good. When a fine, upstanding man is caught doing something wrong, we say, 'There's a good man gone bad.'"

Paul leaned toward me. "Since people did not acknowledge God, he gave them up to a depraved mind to do what should not be done." — *Romans 1:28*

"So actually, I guess we should say, 'There's a bad man found out.'"

Paul leaned closer. "They are filled with all kinds of wickedness, evil, greed, malice. Full of envy, murder, strife, treachery, evil dispositions—" — *Romans 1:29*

"Of course, that probably should include women too," I said. "A bad woman found out."

Paul kept talking and leaning nearer, almost knocking over his cup. "—back-biters, slanderers, haters of God, arrogant, boastful. Devising new evils." — *Romans 1:30*

"Once when I was talking about God showing me how sinful I was, a lady shouted, 'We're not that bad!'"

Romans 1:31

Paul was still going. "Disobedient to parents, foolish, faithless, unloving, without mercy."

"As I recall, she was quite offended."

Romans 3:11

"There is not one who understands," Paul concluded, leaning back in his chair. "Not one who seeks after God."

Jeremiah 17:9

I climbed on the bandwagon. "The Bible says the human heart is desperately wicked. And deceitful above all things."

Galatians 3:22

"Scripture has consigned all under sin so the promised blessing may be given to those who believe in Jesus Christ."

"Still," I said, "it's a pretty sad picture of humanity. And until then our sin separates us from God."

Ephesians 4:17–18

Paul looked over his shoulder and turned back to me, lowering his voice. "They're walking in the futility of their mind. Their understanding is darkened"—Paul gestured with his hand—"totally cut off from the life of God."

"But they don't know it," I said.

"Because of their ignorance."

"Maybe they don't want to know."

"Due to their hardness of heart," Paul said.

In Bondage to Sin

As we talked, the sun slipped behind a cloud, drawing a shadow like a heavy shroud across the room.

"But originally," I said, "mankind was perfect. Before there was sin."

"Sin came into the world through one man," said Paul.

"Yes, Adam—well, and Eve too. Disobeying God in the garden of Eden."

Romans 5:19

"And through that disobedience," Paul said, "the whole human race was made sinful."

"Their very first son was a murderer." I tapped my Bible. "Cain. He killed his brother." *Genesis 4:8*

"Therefore," Paul said, "just as sin came into the world through one man, and through sin came death"—Paul drew a pointed finger across the entire room—"so also, death spread to all mankind because all sinned." *Romans 5:12*

"And ever since then we've been trying to fix ourselves," I said. "By ourselves."

"But I am of the flesh," Paul said.

"Exactly," I said. "All of us are."

"Sold under the authority of sin." *Romans 7:14*

"Starting with that first birth," I said, "everyone born into this world has the sin defect."

"Indeed," said Paul. "I do not even understand my own actions."

"None of us do," I said, "because we are ignorant of the fatal defect deep within us."

"For what I want to do—I don't do it," Paul said. "Instead, I find myself doing the very things I hate." *Romans 7:15*

"You and everybody else."

"But if I do what I do not want to do, that means it is no longer I who do it, but sin which is in me." *Romans 7:16–17*

"Look deep enough," I said, "and you'll see sin prowling the darkened hallways of your heart."

"I know there is no good thing in me—in my flesh," Paul said, "because I want to do what is right but I am not able to do it." *Romans 7:18*

"Now that's a good test right there," I said. "To prove you have the sin defect."

"For I do not do the good things I want to do, but I keep doing the evil things I do not want to do!" *Romans 7:19*

"Exactly." I patted my Bible. "As the prophet said, 'Can a leopard change its spots? Neither can those who do evil start doing good.'" *Jeremiah 13:23*

Romans 7:20

"Again," said Paul, "if I do the things I do not want to do, it is not me doing it, but it is sin within me."

"That's my point," I said. "We are born with the sin defect. And trying to take it out of ourselves would be like…well, like trying to take the pork out of a pig!"

Romans 7:21

"I find that when I want to do what is right, evil is right there with me!"

"Or taking the wood out of a tree—"

Romans 7:22–23

"In my inner self I delight in the law of God. But I see a different force in my body which takes me captive to the power of sin." Paul was getting into a rhythm.

"—or taking the music out of a song." And so was I.

"With my mind I serve the laws of God, but with my flesh I end up serving the power of sin!"

"You cannot take the Adam out of the man!"

Romans 7:24

"Oh, wretched man that I am!" Paul lurched forward. "Who will deliver me from this body of sin and death?"

Now that is the cry of a man who has seen the depths of his own depravity. "Only God can do that," I said. "Take the Adam out of the man."

Romans 7:25

"Thanks be to God!" Paul cried out, falling back into his chair. "Thanks be to God," he said again. "There is deliverance through Jesus Christ our Lord."

And this is the cry of a man who has seen the glorious truth of the gospel.

The room was as still as a sanctuary. I let Paul sit there for a moment, and then I asked, "How is it deliverance?"

Romans 8:2

"The power of the life-giving Spirit in Jesus Christ has set me free." Paul looked up at me. "Free from the power of sin and death."

"It's a dreadful thing, isn't it?" I said. "That power of sin. We're all trapped in it."

I took a look around as people reflected on that. The stone house was starting to remind me of Paul—plain, practical, solid. I caught a glimpse of a small courtyard through the window.

"It's true," Paul began, "we ourselves were once foolish and disobedient…deceived." He looked down at his hands. "Slaves to all kinds of passions and lusts. Full of envy and malice. Hated and hating others."

Titus 3:3

"And speaking of that," I said, "a lot of people say their sins are too great for God to forgive them."

"But the grace of God has now appeared," said Paul, "bringing salvation to all mankind."

Titus 2:11

"And then they ask if God could forgive Hitler."

Paul raised an eyebrow.

"He killed a lot of Jews," I said.

"I killed a lot of Jews."

Acts 7:58, 9:21

"He killed…a lot of Jews."

"But where sin abounded," Paul said, "God's grace overflowed greater still."

Romans 5:20

"Yes!" I lifted my hand high. "God's boundless mercy." I waved my hand across the room. "Toward all who sin."

"And there is no greater sinner than I," Paul said.

1 Timothy 1:15

"You keep saying that."

"Because mercy was given to me, the chief of sinners."

"In other words," I said, "if God can forgive you, he can forgive anybody."

"It was for Jesus Christ to demonstrate his patience," Paul said, "as an example to those who would believe in him and receive eternal life."

1 Timothy 1:16

"What about those with sins piled sky-high?" I had noticed that some of those listening to us were looking down. "What would you say to people like that?"

"Do not despise God's mercy. Or his patience." Paul looked across the room. "Not realizing that his kindness is meant to lead you to repentance."

Romans 2:4

"You keep saying that too," I said. "It sounds like an altar call."

"Altar call?"

"Calling people to repent."

"Everyone who calls on the name of the Lord will be saved."

Romans 10:13

True Repentance

I saw this as my chance to get Paul talking about repentance. There can be a lot of confusion about what it means to repent, and I hoped he could bring some clarity to the whole thing.

I looked at Paul. "Some people think repentance means to feel sorry for the wrong things they've done."

"If it is a godly sorrow," Paul said, "it will produce a repentance that leads to salvation." His eyes were locked on mine. "Never to be regretted."

2 Corinthians 7:10

So sorrow can *lead* to repentance. I rubbed the back of my neck. We would have to dig some more at this one. "Does a godly sorrow see sin the way God sees it?"

"A godly grief will produce a desire to forsake the sin," Paul said, "and a longing to make things right."

2 Corinthians 7:11

"I've heard of drunkards weeping and wailing over the jobs they lost and families they destroyed"—I mimicked bringing a bottle to my mouth—"but they refused to stop drinking."

"That's a worldly sorrow," Paul said. "It produces only death."

"How does it produce death?"

"The wages of sin is death." Paul shrugged. "And they remain in their sin."

Romans 6:23

"But deep down we all know sin is wrong," I said. "Because we hide it. Lie about it...make excuses."

"There must be a sense of distress and anguish that recognizes the wickedness of sin."

"Like when you cried out to be delivered from your body of death?"

"A godly sorrow creates that kind of fear and deep concern. Even anger at sin." *2 Corinthians 7:11*

"And without that people won't let go of their sin," I said. "I guess that's why God's prophets told people to weep and wail and mourn at their sin." *Joel 2:12*

"And it is why Jesus sent me to open their eyes—"

"To the truth!" I said. "To see sin as the evil, soul-destroying thing it is!"

"—so they may turn from darkness to light and from the power of Satan to God."

"Yes, turn from sin," I said. "Renounce it. That's the true repentance!"

"So they may receive forgiveness of their sins," Paul said. *Acts 26:17–18*

"The Bible says whoever confesses and forsakes their sins will receive mercy." *Proverbs 28:13*

"Just as I proclaimed at the beginning to those at Damascus," Paul said. "Repent and turn to God, doing works in keeping with repentance." *Acts 26:20*

"James said that too. He said to grieve and mourn and weep over sin…and draw near to God." I turned to the group. "And that was a word he sent to believers." *James 4:8–9*

"Do you not know"—Paul smacked the table with his hand—"that when you present yourselves to someone as slaves, you become slaves of the one you obey?" He raised his hand again. "Either of sin which leads to death—" *Romans 6:16*

"Just like God warned Israel," I said, hitting the table before Paul could. "Turn, turn from your wicked ways! For why will you die?" *Ezekiel 33:11*

"For distress and despair"—Paul whacked the table again—"will fall upon every person who persists in evil." *Romans 2:9*

The World's Greatest Recall

I could sense the frustration in Paul—in God too—like a parent warning a loved, but disobedient, child. I said, "It makes you angry, doesn't it?"

Romans 14:10, 12

"Because we all will stand before the judgment seat of God." Paul swept up everyone in the room with one frightful sweep of his hand. "And each one of us will have to render an account of himself to God."

"Scary."

2 Corinthians 5:11

"Therefore, knowing the fear of the Lord, we are trying to persuade people."

"Well, with respect, Paul, I think you will persuade more flies with honey than vinegar."

Galatians 1:10

"Am I now trying to win the approval of men?" Paul said. "Or of God!" He flung his arms wide. "Am I seeking to please men?"

"OK, I'm not sure how we landed here, but—"

"If I were still trying to please men, I should not be a servant of Christ."

"It just sounds to me like you're preaching the law," I said. "Do this—don't do that."

Galatians 1:4

"Christ gave himself for our sins." Paul tapped the table with his finger. "To rescue us from this evil age."

"Not sure I see the connection."

Paul sat there—very still. Staring at me. Waiting.

"Of course!" I said. "If we don't see our sin, how can Jesus rescue us from it?"

As usual, Paul had been way ahead of me. But I did catch up. "And to talk only about Jesus and his salvation," I said, "would be like throwing a life preserver to people on the dock."

Romans 3:20

"It is the law that brings an awareness of sin," Paul said.

"Right," I said. "Get them out into the water. Deep water."

"I personally would not have known what sin is," said Paul, "had not it been for the law."

"For example?"

"If the law did not say, 'Thou shalt not covet,' I would not know what it is to covet." — Romans 7:7

"Like to covet your neighbor's house or car," I said. "Or to lust after—"

"The law showed how intensely sinful sin is." — Romans 7:13

"Just as I said, sin is a very serious defect. And there's no way we can fix it ourselves."

"God desires that everyone should come to a knowledge of the truth and be saved." — 1 Timothy 2:4

"That's surely God's recall notice," I said. "And repentance brings us into God's garage."

Paul's head jerked up.

"To get fixed," I said. "When Jesus began to preach the gospel, that was his very first word. Repent." — Mark 1:15

"Even before Jesus appeared," Paul said, "John the Baptist proclaimed a baptism of repentance to the people of Israel." — Acts 13:24

"And even before that," I said, "God spoke through his prophets, calling his people to repentance. So that's not new."

"But now, God is telling all people everywhere to repent." — Acts 17:30

"Yes, you said that. But you didn't say why."

"Because God has set a day when he will judge the world by a man he has appointed."

"Jesus."

"And God has given everyone a certainty of this by raising him from the dead." — Acts 17:31

"I know people who will want to argue about that," I said. "Any advice?"

"Gently correct those in opposition," Paul said. "Do not quarrel. Be patient." He shrugged again. "Perhaps God might grant them repentance unto a knowledge of the truth—" — 2 Timothy 2:24–25

"Repentance opens the door to the truth."

"—so people may regain their senses and escape the snare of the devil." Paul scowled, but it wasn't at me. "He has taken them captive to do his will."

John 14:6
1 John 3:8

"Jesus said he is the truth." I held up my Bible. "And Scripture says he came to destroy the works of the devil."

2 Timothy 3:15

Paul pointed to my Bible. "Those holy Scriptures can give you the wisdom that leads to salvation through faith in Jesus Christ."

"Faith in Jesus Christ," I said. "So there are two things going on here to get saved."

Paul nodded.

"The first one is repentance," I said. "Turning from sin."

Romans 4:7

"Blessed are those whose wrongdoings have been forgiven." Paul sounded like a recording. He probably had repeated that a thousand times.

"Right," I said. "And the other one, as you just said, is faith in Jesus Christ."

Galatians 2:16

"We are counted righteous only by believing in Jesus Christ"—Paul was nodding his head approvingly—"and knowing this, we have placed our faith in Christ, that we might be declared righteous by believing in him."

"Paul! That was the second word of Jesus when he started preaching! Well, third. He said, 'Repent and believe.'" I leaned across the table. "Believe the good news about him!"

Acts 20:20–21

"Just as I taught publicly and in private." Paul slowly leaned to within an inch of my face. "Earnestly testifying to Jews and others alike—both repentance toward God and faith toward the Lord Jesus Christ."

"Then we need to talk about Jesus!"

3
THE MESSIAH COMES

The Jews had waited centuries for the arrival of their Messiah. He was the anointed one of God who would destroy their enemies and provide salvation for all of mankind. Old Testament prophets said he would bring peace to earth, end pain and suffering, and restore the unspoiled creation that had existed before the fall of Adam and Eve. And one other thing: he would be divine—the Son of God.

When the New Testament writers recorded the gospel, they were sharing the good news that the Messiah had finally come. Writing in Greek, they used the word 'Christos', a translation of the Hebrew word for Messiah, meaning anointed one. From this, we have the English word, Christ. When we see "Jesus, the Christ" in our English Bibles, it means Jesus, the Messiah—the anointed one. Thus Christ is a title, not a name, though it often appears as "Jesus Christ."

The Jewish nation's expectation of their Messiah's appearance had reached a peak at the time of the first century AD. And when John the Baptist began to baptize people in the Jordan River, it started quite a buzz. Perhaps the Messiah had come! The Bible tells us that all the people were wondering in their hearts whether John was the Messiah.

To settle the matter, priests were sent out from Jerusalem to ask him, "Who are you?" John's response was simple and direct. He said, "I am not the Messiah." But John threw fresh fuel on their red-hot hope. He said, "I baptize you with water, but there is one more powerful than I coming. He will baptize you with the Holy Spirit and with fire."

Later, when Jesus of Nazareth appeared on the scene, new rumors arose among the people. At one point in his ministry, Jesus asked his disciples, "Who do people say that I am?" They told him some people thought he was Elijah, or possibly Jeremiah, or one of the other prophets. And this uncertainty about who Jesus was continued.

Even John the Baptist, who had recognized Jesus as the Son of God when he baptized him, began to doubt. He finally sent two of his followers to ask Jesus, "Are you the one who was to come, or are we to look for someone else?" Jesus knew that John the Baptist would be familiar with the Jewish prophecies about the Messiah. So Jesus said, "Go tell John what you have seen and heard: the blind receive their sight, the lame walk, lepers are cleansed, the deaf hear, the dead are raised to life, and the gospel is proclaimed."

Thus, the Bible records that Jesus came to his own people, but they did not recognize him. Some two thousand years later, people continue to argue about who Jesus is, so it is not surprising that it took a while for the first-century Jews and their leaders to sort things out. And this is where I began my conversation with the apostle Paul.

Who is the Messiah?

"Paul, I know there were many who thought John the Baptist was the Messiah. Was that because he was preaching repentance and baptizing people?"

Acts 19:4

"John's baptism was indeed a baptism of repentance," Paul said, "but he told the people they should believe in the one coming after him—that is, in Jesus Christ."

"So you're saying John knew his role. It was to prepare the hearts of the people to receive the Messiah."

Acts 13:23–24

"Yes, and after John had first preached a baptism of repentance, God raised up for Israel a Savior—Jesus."

"But a lot of people still weren't sure."

"True," said Paul. "Even as John was drawing to the end of his ministry, he was saying, 'I am not the Messiah. I am not worthy to untie the sandals of the one coming after me.'"   *Acts 13:25*

"And right to the brutal end of his own ministry, people still doubted Jesus," I said. "They taunted him as he hung on the cross. Even the rulers sneered, 'If he is the Messiah let him save himself.'"   *Luke 23:35*

"The people of Jerusalem did not recognize Jesus," Paul said. "Neither did their leaders."

"Messiah. Savior of the world," I said. "How do you get people to believe it's you?"

"They did not understand the prophecies read every Sabbath."   *Acts 13:27*

"That the Messiah would be pierced for our transgressions and crushed for our iniquities."   *Isaiah 53:5*

Paul nodded.

"And that God would make his Christ an offering for sin…that he would bear our sins."   *Isaiah 53:10–11*

"And because they didn't understand these Scriptures," Paul said, "they fulfilled them by condemning Jesus."

"He was whipped and nailed to a cross, just like the prophets said."   *Mark 15:15*

"The Jews found no grounds at all for putting him to death, yet they demanded his execution from Pilate."   *Acts 13:28*

"Quite an irony," I said, "because his death won salvation for the very Jews who condemned him."

"And the Gentiles."

"The whole world."

"All creation," Paul said. "His resurrection proved it."   *Colossians 1:20*
Romans 4:25

"We might be getting ahead of ourselves." I looked around. People were still working their way in and sitting down.

"But that is my gospel!" Paul said. "Jesus the Messiah—raised from the dead."   *2 Timothy 2:8*

"Well then, let's unpack your gospel."

Paul gave me a blank stare.

"Talk about it," I said, tilting my head toward Paul. "Explain it?"

Romans 1:2 Paul needed very little prompting on that one—he dove right in. "It is the good news God promised long ago through his prophets about his Son, Jesus Christ."

"The Messiah."

Romans 1:3 "He was born of King David's family line."

"That means he is human"—I made a slow, broad flourish—"like the rest of us."

Romans 1:4 "And he was revealed as the Son of God in power by the Holy Spirit," Paul said, "by his resurrection from the dead."

"And that means he is divine," I said. "Like God."

Paul smiled. "He is the very image of the invisible God. And everything in the heavens and on earth was created in him. The visible and the invisible—"

Genesis 1:1 "Wait a minute," I said. "The very first sentence of the Bible says God created the heavens and the earth."

Colossians 1:15–16 "I said *in* him all things were created. Everything was created through him and for him."

"So the Jesus who walked on earth was God," I said. "In the flesh."

Colossians 1:19 "Yes. Because in him all the fullness of God was pleased to dwell, and—"

"Fully man and fully God."

Paul paused and looked at me. I immediately resolved to stop interrupting him.

"—and through him," Paul continued, "God would restore all things to himself—"

"All things?" I said. Oops. But I wasn't trying to be rude. I was just excited.

"—all things," Paul said, "whether on earth or in heaven—"

"That's why you said he saved all creation!" Plus, I wanted us all to get this right.

Colossians 1:20 "—by making peace through his blood shed on the cross."

"The blood of Christ," I said. "No ordinary blood, I'm sure. But how, I mean why—"

"It was God's eternal plan," Paul said. "To bring all things together again in Christ. Things in heaven and things on earth." *Ephesians 1:10*

"Everything that was severed by sin—all gathered together in the Messiah!"

"Indeed," said Paul, "all creation has been groaning in labor pains to this very hour." *Romans 8:22*

"Labor pains?"

"One day," Paul said, "all creation itself will be delivered from its bondage to decay and death into the glorious freedom of the children of God." *Romans 8:21*

"Talk about a new birth!" I said. "And to think God planned to do all this through Jesus."

"His own Son," Paul said. *Acts 9:20*

"So all this didn't just"—I waved a hand in the air—"you know, happen out of the blue."

"At the prearranged time," Paul said, "God sent forth his Son to be born of a woman to redeem those who were under law."

"The Jews," I said, "and all their laws."

"That we might be adopted as children." *Galatians 4:4–5*

"The Messiah of the Jews," I said.

Paul's face reddened. "Can it be that God is the God only of the Jews?"

"I meant the Messiah of Jewish prophecy."

"Is he not also the God of the Gentiles?"

"Jewish prophecy," I said, "but for the Gentiles too."

"Most assuredly the Gentiles also," said Paul, "since there is only one God. And he will pronounce those who are circumcised righteous by faith—and also those who are uncircumcised through the same faith." *Romans 3:29–30*

"I wasn't saying—"

Paul's hand shot up like a stop sign on a dirt road. "So the Gentiles would be co-heirs with us. And we all share in God's promise in Christ through the gospel." *Ephesians 3:6*

"And that is great!" I said. "So can we get back to Christ's mission?"

"That *was* Christ's mission!" Paul said. "By means of his cross to reconcile both Jews and Gentiles to God, united in one body." *Ephesians 2:16*

"I mean can we go back to where you were talking about God sending forth his Son?"

"Of course," said Paul. "Though the divine nature was Christ's from the beginning—"

"Before time." I looked at Paul and mouthed the words, "Just helping."

"—Christ emptied himself." Paul shook his head. "And taking the nature of a servant, he was born in the likeness of men." *Philippians 2:6–7*

"The God-man," I said. "It's hard to really get hold of that sometimes."

"It is a great mystery," said Paul. "God appeared in the flesh, was seen by angels, and proclaimed to the nations. He was believed on in the world and taken up in glory—" *1 Timothy 3:16*

"Paul, we're losing folks here," I interrupted, noticing some puzzled faces. "Could we go back, ah…"

"And being found in human form"—Paul quickly readjusted—"Christ humbled himself, becoming obedient unto death. Even to death on the cross." *Philippians 2:8*

"People struggle with that too," I said. "The Savior of the world coming to earth to die."

"I know," said Paul. "I spent three Sabbaths in a Jewish synagogue in Thessalonica explaining and showing from the Scriptures that the Messiah had to suffer and rise again from the dead."

Paul ran his fingers through his hair. "And I told them, 'This Jesus I proclaim to you, he is the promised Messiah.'" *Acts 17:2–3*

God's Secret Plan

I knew that the Jews had struggled to connect all their prophecies about the Messiah with Jesus. "Paul, I think a lot of Jews expected the Messiah to be their political savior. You know, big army, deliver them from their enemies. Especially Rome."

"To this day I have testified to great and small alike"—Paul waved his hand toward all those around us—"saying nothing beyond what the prophets and Moses said would happen." *Acts 26:22*

"Which is?"

"That the Messiah must suffer and die—"

"If they see that Jesus is both God and man, the great and small alike will understand."

"—and that he would be the first to rise from the dead," said Paul. *Acts 26:23*

"OK, there's a new one," I said. "Because everybody dies…and stays dead. From the beginning of time."

"But this," Paul said, tapping the table, "this is in accordance with God's plan in Jesus Christ before time even began." *2 Timothy 1:9*

"You mean God's hidden plan to give eternal life to mankind?"

"Now revealed by the appearing of Jesus Christ, our Savior."

"Still, people are afraid to die," I said. "It seems so final."

"Death is the last enemy to be overthrown." *1 Corinthians 15:26*

"We don't usually see somebody who died walking around. It'd be quite a news story."

Paul jumped to his feet, knocking his water cup to the floor. "Christ! Destroyed! Death!" He sheared off each word, his hand falling like the blade of a guillotine.

"Quite a headline!" I looked up at Paul. "But the storyline is that even Christ died."

"And he has now brought life and immortality to light through the gospel," Paul said, adding gravely, "which I was appointed to preach and teach." *2 Timothy 1:10–11*

"Yet people are still physically dying," I said, "while you preach eternal life."

2 Corinthians 5:1 — "Because we know that if this"—Paul looked down at his body—"this…tent which is our earthly home is destroyed, we have an eternal house from God in the heavens."

"So perhaps we could say death no longer has the last word."

1 Corinthians 6:14 — "Just as God has raised up Jesus," said Paul, "he will also raise us up by his power."

"And now life has the last word." I picked up Paul's cup and set it back on the table. "But it's too bad Christ had to die."

1 Corinthians 15:21 — Paul straightened his chair and sat down. "Since death came by a man, the resurrection of the dead also came by a man."

"Adam plunged us into sin and separation from God," I said, "and Jesus died for our sin to bring us back to God."

Romans 5:21 — "Just as sin reigned in death," Paul said, nodding and smiling, "in the same way grace will reign through righteousness unto eternal life because of Christ."

"Speaking of righteousness, didn't the Jews believe the Messiah would enable them to fulfill their law?"

Romans 10:4 — "Yes, but Christ himself is the fulfillment of the law," Paul said, "so righteousness may be attained by everyone who believes in him."

Matthew 5:20 — "Jesus said our righteousness would have to surpass the scribes and Pharisees to enter the kingdom of heaven."

"But now a divine righteousness is revealed—quite apart from the law." Paul looked around the room. "And it is given to all through faith in Jesus Christ."

"So how could the Jewish leaders miss that?" I said. "A way to be right with God apart from the law."

Romans 10:2 — "They have a great zeal for God," Paul said, "but they are not guided by true knowledge."

Matthew 15:14 — "Jesus said they were blind." I walked my fingers clumsily across the table. "Blind leading the blind, as Jesus put it. Right into the ditch."

"And being ignorant of the righteousness from God"—Paul slowly shook his head—"and trying to achieve their own through the law, they did not submit to God's plan." *Romans 10:3*

"So no righteousness for them," I said.

"And why?" Paul said. "Because they sought it through works rather than through faith."

"And that's the faith you keep talking about."

"Yes," Paul said. "They stumbled at the stumbling stone." *Romans 9:32*

"They tripped over Jesus," I said. "The Jews didn't believe he was the Messiah, so they missed out on God's free righteousness." I saw several people nod crisply at that one.

Paul must have noticed too. "My friends," he said, "in case you should think too highly of yourselves, I want you to know that a partial blindness has come upon Israel." He glanced around the room. "And it will continue only until the full number of the Gentiles has been gathered in." *Romans 11:25*

"So start believing in Jesus," I said. "And tell your friends!"

"As Scripture says, 'See, I am laying a stumbling stone in Zion—but the one who believes in him will not be put to shame.'" *Romans 9:33*

"Our shame is our sin."

"For we all have sinned," Paul said, "but through the redemption in Jesus Christ we are freely declared righteous." *Romans 3:23–24*

I saw a few furrowed brows. "Redemption?"

"God sent Jesus as an atoning sacrifice by the shedding of his blood." Paul nodded toward the group. "To be received through faith." *Romans 3:25*

"OK," I said. "Now I just want to make sure we're all clear on this." I held up a finger. "Everybody on earth has this sin defect."

"It is true. For God has given everyone over to disobedience that he may show mercy to all." *Romans 11:32*

"That's my next point." I held up two fingers. "God loves us, and he sent his Son to pay for our sin so he can forgive us."

Paul nodded again.

I held up three fingers. "But we have to recognize our own sin and turn from it."

Paul nodded once more, but I could tell he was getting impatient.

"Last one." Four fingers. "We also need to believe in Jesus and his death for us. And of course, accept him as our—"

Romans 3:28

"Therefore," Paul interrupted, "we maintain that a person is pronounced righteous by God through faith alone and not by obedience to the law."

"But before we can have faith in Jesus as our Savior," I said, "we have to know who he is and what he did for us."

"If with your mouth," said Paul, "you declare that Jesus is Lord—"

"And also why he did it," I said, "come to think of it."

Romans 10:9

"—and believe in your heart that God raised him from the dead, you shall be saved."

"That's what people who have doubts ask," I said. "Why would God raise Jesus from the dead?"

"Jesus was given up to death because of our trespasses."

"Right, I think we all got that part."

Romans 4:25

"And he was raised to life because of our being declared righteous."

"As proof that all our sins have been forgiven!"

Acts 16:31

"Just as we said to the jailer at Philippi"—Paul was grinning like a schoolboy—"'Believe in the Lord Jesus Christ, and you shall be saved.'"

That Elusive Faith

A cheerful murmur rippled through the room as people smiled at each other and affirmed Paul's gleeful declaration. "Still," I said, "sometimes it's pretty hard getting people to believe in Jesus. That he's the Messiah." The ripple subsided.

"You have been saved through faith," Paul said. "But it is not of you. It is a gift of God." *Ephesians 2:8–9*

I fingered my Bible. "When Peter said to Jesus, 'You are the Messiah, the Son of God,' Jesus said, 'Blessed are you, for no one has revealed this to you but my Father in heaven.'" *Matthew 16:16–17*

Paul looked around the room, nodding and pointing. "And that is the same Jesus, the Son of God we proclaimed to you. He is our Savior, the Lord Jesus Christ." *2 Corinthians 1:19* / *Titus 1:4*

"If people won't believe Jesus is the Messiah," I said, "they certainly won't believe he's the Son of God." I leaned back in my chair. "Let alone Savior." I looked over to Paul. "Not to mention Lord."

Paul leaned toward me. "It is only by the Holy Spirit that anyone can say Jesus is Lord." *1 Corinthians 12:3*

"Why is that?"

"Because faith comes from hearing. And hearing comes from the word of God." *Romans 10:17*

"Faith comes from hearing the good news about Jesus?" I said. "I'm afraid that doesn't always work."

"Not everyone responds to the gospel." *Romans 10:16*

"It's as though they don't really hear it. They just can't get it."

"But if the gospel we bring is veiled," Paul said, "it is hidden to those who are perishing." *2 Corinthians 4:3*

"Perishing? As in, like…dying?"

"As in the day when God will judge the secrets of everyone through Jesus Christ." *Romans 2:16*

"Paul, that's awful! How is it hidden? Why can't they see it?"

"The god of this age has blinded the minds of unbelievers."

"Satan!"

"So they cannot see the illuminating light from the gospel," Paul said.

"So they can't see the truth and get saved," I said. "So they can't see—"

_{2 Corinthians 4:4}

"The glory and majesty of Christ, who is the very image of God."

"I think there's something Satan doesn't want people to know," I said.

_{2 Corinthians 5:18}

"That God has reconciled us to himself through Jesus Christ."

"The Bible says God was *in* Christ."

_{Colossians 2:9}

"Truly, all the fullness of the Godhead dwells bodily in the Christ."

"Though I'm still trying to absorb that," I said. "All of God in Jesus."

_{Romans 5:6, 8}

"That is how God showed his love for us," said Paul, "in that Christ died for us while we were helpless sinners."

"Paul, I just had a thought!" I sat bolt upright. "Since Jesus is the Son of God—you know, God in the flesh—that means, well, it means…"

_{Acts 20:28}

"God bought his church with his own blood." Paul didn't even flinch when he said that.

But I did. "God himself…on the cross," I said softly. I had never thought of it that way.

I pushed myself up from the table. "I think I have to step outside."

It was late, and almost everyone had already trickled away with the sunlight. But the night sky was so ablaze with starlight and a full moon that it could have been noon. I sat down on one of the stone benches. It was still warm.

I had to process this. Just as a car manufacturer covers the cost to fix a defective automobile, God—our maker—covers the cost to fix us. And that cost is blood. The blood of his Son. Or as Paul put it, "his own blood."

I shivered.

Paul came outside and joined me on the bench, looking at the stars.

"I've been thinking," I said. "The one thing Jesus died for…was our sin."

"God made him who never knew sin to be sin for us."

I turned to Paul. "And now he wants to take all our sins from us and set us free."

Paul's gaze settled on me. "That we might become the righteousness of God in Christ." *2 Corinthians 5:21*

I looked down and was surprised to see I was holding my Bible, gripping it like a lifeline. I opened it, found the words of the prophet Isaiah, and read, "We all like sheep have gone astray. Everyone has turned to his own way. And God has laid on him the iniquity of us all." *Isaiah 53:6*

I looked at Paul. "We are so wicked."

"But God is rich in mercy," Paul said, "because of the great love he has for us." *Ephesians 2:4*

"He lifts us from the depths of depravity to the heights of glory."

Paul stood and looked up to the heavens. "Yes, even though we were dead in sin he made us alive together with Christ." *Ephesians 2:5*

"Look at that sky," I said. "All those stars." I skimmed the vast night sky. "And to think God's love is bigger than all of that."

I stood up and stepped closer to Paul. "Hard to wrap your head around it."

Paul stared up at me. "And I am convinced that nothing can separate us from that love."

"That's even harder to grasp."

"Not death, nor life, nor angelic powers. And neither things present nor things to come." Paul slowly scanned the heavens from horizon to horizon. "And neither height nor depth… *Romans 8:38–39* nothing in all creation can separate us from the love of God in our Lord Jesus Christ."

"Nothing, Paul?"

"Nothing."

"Why is that?"

2 Corinthians 5:17

"Because you"—Paul smiled and gently poked me in the chest with his finger—"you are a new creation."

"A new creation." I definitely would have to get Paul to unpack that one.

4
A New and Improved You

One of the most powerful words in advertising is the little word "new." We love new. Perhaps it's our fascination with novelty—fresh, different, something that never existed before. "New" sells a lot of stuff.

Another potent advertising word is "improved." It's right up there with "new" in peddling power. If something is improved, it must be better than before and therefore more desirable. When you put these two words together, you have a real powerhouse. Now, God is not in the advertising business. But he is in the new and improved business. And as it turns out, new and improved is a perfect description of the born-again you. Let me explain.

When you first entered this world, you were a new creation born of your mom and dad. You were a completely new life that had never existed before. Pretty exciting! But unfortunately, you were born with a flaw, a deadly defect inherited from your parents. It was passed down to you from Adam and Eve, the first couple on earth. It is called sin, and it separates you from God. That's the bad news. But the good news is that God has provided a way to fix that sin defect and reunite you with him!

Nicodemus, a Pharisee and a ruler of the Jews, had a little chat about this with Jesus Christ some two thousand years ago. Nicodemus believed that Jesus had come from God because, as he said, "No one could perform such miraculous signs unless God were with him." Jesus replied that no one can enter into the kingdom of God unless he is born again.

Nicodemus, stuck in the physical realm like many people today, wondered aloud how someone could enter his mother's womb a second time and be born again! Jesus explained he was talking about a spiritual birth. He said a person must be born from above; that is, born of the Holy Spirit to see God's kingdom and enter into it.

As Jesus put it, "What is born of the flesh is flesh, and what is born of the Spirit is spirit." In other words, the fleshly you is born of the flesh, born of your earthly parents into this world. The spiritual you is born of the Spirit, born of your heavenly Father into the kingdom of God.

But someone may ask, "Why would anyone want to enter the kingdom of God?" Why indeed! Because that is where God resides! God is Spirit, and the kingdom of God is the spiritual realm of his unbroken presence and power. Who wouldn't want to be a part of that?

This spiritual birth Jesus spoke of is a brand-new creation. It is a brand-new life. And just as you grew up in your physical life—learning first how to crawl, then to walk and then run—you also need to grow and develop in your spiritual life. Everyone born of God needs to learn about this new and improved creation. What is its nature? How does it work?

I decided that would be my first question for Paul during this session: "What are we?" I was sure Paul would say we're a new creation. That would be a good starting point to explore this new life that comes from God.

A New Creation

"Paul, there's an old saying among Christians, 'Become what you are.'" I leaned across the table toward him. "So I guess the question is, what are we, exactly?"

"We are all sons of God," Paul said.

"Paul, I think…I thought we were going to talk about a new creation."

Paul started to say something, then stopped and stared at me.

"OK," I said. "Sons of God it is. That's a good place to start too."

"Through faith in Jesus Christ." Paul waved his hand around the room. "For all of you who were baptized into Christ have put on Christ." *Galatians 3:26–27*

"Baptized into Christ?" I said. "Put on Christ?"

"By one Spirit we were all baptized into one body."

"The body of Christ?"

"So we, although many"—Paul gestured to the room—"we are one body in Christ."

I saw a few people frown and turn to each other. "Paul, can you break that down a bit?"

"In this way"—Paul brought his hands together, fingers intertwined—"by our union in Christ, although we are many, we form but one body." He wiggled his fingers. "And individually we are connected one to another as its parts." *Romans 12:5*

"That helps…a bit."

"And we were all given of one Spirit to drink." *1 Corinthians 12:13*

"Paul, I—" This was moving way too fast. I took a breath and exhaled slowly. "When was that?"

"When you heard the good news of salvation, you trusted in Christ?" Paul raised his voice at the end to make it a question.

"Yes. I did."

"Having believed in him"—Paul brought his hands together again, this time with one clasping the other—"you were sealed as his by receiving the Holy Spirit." *Ephesians 1:13*

"So it's a spiritual thing." I still wanted to get to the new creation.

"So now you are the body of Christ"—Paul's hand swept out again—"and all of you members of it." *1 Corinthians 12:27*

"Jesus is the Son of God," I said, "and if we are his body, that would make us a part of God's family."

"All those who are guided by the Spirit of God"—Paul looked around the room—"these are the sons of God." *Romans 8:14*

"And daughters." I nodded slightly toward a young woman seated near us.

Romans 8:16 — "The Holy Spirit himself," said Paul, "testifies with our spirit that we are children of God."

Very sensitive of Paul, I thought, picking up on that sons and daughters thing.

Romans 8:19 — "And all of creation waits with eager expectation," Paul said, "for the revealing of the sons of God."

"Oops," I said. "The daughters too."

2 Corinthians 6:16, 18 — "As God himself has said"—Paul looked at my Bible and then at me—"'I will be your Father, and you will be my sons and my daughters.'"

I stared at my Bible, wondering why I was trying to teach Paul twenty-first century political correctness.

"Says the Lord God Almighty," Paul added, with a no-frills finality.

"So why is all creation waiting for the revealing of the sons and—"

Romans 8:21 — "Because then"—Paul didn't miss a beat—"creation itself will be delivered from its bonds of decay into the glorious freedom of the children of God."

"OK, we're all over the map here," I said. "And I do want to hear about our glorious future, but I wanted to talk a bit about our new creation now. You know, new and improved!"

2 Corinthians 5:17 — Paul reached over and laid his hand on mine. "If anyone is in Christ"—he squeezed my hand—"there is a new creation."

"How so?"

1 Corinthians 6:17 — "Anyone who is joined to the Lord becomes one spirit with him," Paul said.

"My spirit united with the Spirit of Jesus," I echoed Paul. "That's a new creation!"

"Created after the likeness of God."

"The new and improved me!"

"The new self," Paul said, "created in true righteousness and holiness." *Ephesians 4:24*

"But what of the old me?" I said. "The defective me—steeped in sin?"

"The old things have passed away."

"Old things?"

"Our old self," Paul said triumphantly, "was crucified with Christ!"

"I was crucified with Christ?"

"I am convinced he died for all," Paul said, "therefore all died." *2 Corinthians 5:14*

"Ah, yes, you mentioned that earlier," I said. "All died…I wanted to ask about that."

"This we know," said Paul, "that our old self was crucified with Christ to render the body of sin powerless." He waved his hand toward the group. "So we would no longer be enslaved to sin." *Romans 6:6*

"And how does the death of our old self do that?"

"Because anyone who has died has been freed from sin." *Romans 6:7*

"But how, Paul?" I looked around the room. "We need to know how."

"What the law could not do because our flesh is weak, God did by sending his Son in the likeness of sinful flesh to atone for sin." *Romans 8:3*

I nodded. "We know about forgiveness, but how are we set free from sin?"

"God condemned sin in the flesh," Paul said, "depriving sin of its power over us."

"Deprived sin of its power," I said. Now we were getting somewhere. "And how did he do that, exactly?"

Paul settled back into his chair and slipped into his teaching mode, slow and steady. "In Christ you were circumcised by putting off the body of the flesh." *Colossians 2:11*

"Circumcision seems to keep coming up."

"It was not done with hands." Paul shook his head. "Outward bodily circumcision is not the real circumcision." *Romans 2:28*

"So what's the real circumcision?"

Romans 2:29 — "The real circumcision is of the heart." Paul's hand sliced across his chest. "By the Spirit."

Ezekiel 36:26 — "Ouch." I looked at Paul and pointed to my Bible. "But God did promise that one day he would give people a new heart. Something about removing our heart of stone and giving us a heart of flesh."

"It is the circumcision of Christ," Paul said.

"And you say it's by the Holy Spirit." I nodded, as did a few others. "So it is spiritual."

Colossians 2:13 — "Although you were dead in your sins and your uncircumcised flesh," Paul said, "God made you alive together with Christ."

"Spiritually alive." I nodded again. "By our union with Christ."

"Having forgiven you all of your sins," Paul added, with a lingering emphasis on "all."

I appreciated Paul's focus on the forgiveness of sins, but I wanted to get back to the other half of the equation. "So can you just remind us why we don't have to sin anymore?"

Romans 8:2 — "Because the power of the Holy Spirit has set you free from the power of sin." Paul slapped the table. "And of death!" he said, striking the table again. A little harder than necessary in my view, and for a moment I wondered if Paul was mad at sin, death, or me. But it drove home his point.

"You mean, like, I really don't have to sin anymore?"

2 Corinthians 5:17 — "Behold!" Paul looked at me, smiled, and spread his hands outward. "The new has come!"

"New and improved!"

Romans 6:14 — "Sin is no longer your master."

I felt like dancing.

Spiritual Secrets

Sunlight flooded into the room through the large, open windows. It was as though a gloriously bright light had suddenly been switched on.

"Why is all that so hard for people to get, Paul?"

"Who can really know your thoughts except your own spirit which is in you?"

"Well, nobody, I guess." I glanced up. "Thank goodness. But that doesn't really answer—"

"In the same way, no one knows the things of God," Paul said, "except his Spirit." 1 Corinthians 2:11

"Oh, well that makes sense. So nobody really knows God's mind."

"And yet we speak of the hidden, secret wisdom of God—" 1 Corinthians 2:7

"How is that?"

"God revealed these things to us through his Spirit"—Paul wove his finger through the air—"for the Spirit probes all things." He turned to look at me. "Even the deep things of God." 1 Corinthians 2:10

I nodded. "The Spirit of God reveals the things of God."

"And we have received the Spirit sent from God so we can understand what God has given us." 1 Corinthians 2:12

"The deeper you go into the gospel," I said, "the closer you get to God. That's what I'm finding."

"And we speak of these things not in words of human wisdom, but in the wisdom taught by the Spirit." Paul motioned with his fingers as though unraveling something. "Explaining spiritual truths to spiritual men." 1 Corinthians 2:13

"Spiritual truths of the spiritual realm."

"But the natural man rejects this teaching of the Spirit of God." Paul pointed to his head. "For to him it is foolishness. He cannot grasp it"— Paul pointed to his heart—"because it is understood only by spiritual insight." 1 Corinthians 2:14

"And that's why people don't get it when we try to tell them spiritual things!"

1 Corinthians 2:15 — "But the person with spiritual insight can understand everything." Paul looked down toward the table, his face taut. "Although he himself is not understood by those of the world."

"Yes!" I said, tapping the table, "it'd be like talking to this table."

"For who has understood the mind of the Lord…" Paul's voice trailed off, tracking down a distant memory.

Mark 4:23 — "Who indeed?" I said. "Whenever Jesus talked about the kingdom of God, he cried out, 'Whoever has ears to hear, let them hear!'"

1 Corinthians 2:16 — Paul looked at me. "But we have the mind of Christ."

"So can we talk about the kingdom of God?" I asked.

1 Corinthians 4:20 — "The kingdom of God is not based on words, but on power."

"OK then, let's talk about power," I said. Even better.

1 Corinthians 2:4 — "My gospel and my preaching were not just with persuasive words," Paul said, "but with a display of the Spirit and of power."

John 3:3 — "Jesus said we must be born again to see the kingdom of God."

Titus 3:4–5 — "True, and when the grace of God and his love for us appeared," Paul said, looking around the room, "he saved us by the washing of rebirth and renewing by the Holy Spirit."

"New and improved," I said, "with Holy Spirit power."

2 Corinthians 4:7 — "But we have this treasure in these earthen vessels." Paul gestured to his body. "That the surpassing power may be seen to come from God and not from us."

"Wow," I said. "God's power in me. Hard to believe sometimes."

1 Corinthians 3:16 — "Do you not know you are a temple of God," Paul said, "and his Spirit dwells in you?"

"Yes, but I think you can know something without really… knowing it."

Ephesians 1:19 — "Oh, that you would know the unlimited greatness of his power to us who believe!"

"Unlimited?"

"It is the same mighty power God worked in Christ when he raised him from the dead." Paul lifted both hands upwards. "And sat him at his right hand on high." *Ephesians 1:20*

"I bet we tap into less than one billionth of that power." I shook my head. "Just too timid to ask, I guess."

"God did not give us a spirit of timidity," said Paul, "but a spirit of power, love, and self-control." *2 Timothy 1:7*

"Jesus had all those things," I said, "and we are joined to his Spirit."

"For you have received the Spirit of adoption." *Romans 8:15*

"Yes, we did," I said, looking around. "Sons and daughters of God."

"And because you are sons, God sent into your hearts the Spirit of his own Son with the cry, 'Abba, Father.'" *Galatians 4:6*

"So there's actually a lot more going on here than the forgiveness of sins."

Paul leaned close to me, as though to share something precious. "It is the secret hidden for ages and generations, but now revealed to God's saints." *Colossians 1:26*

"To his holy ones."

"God revealed to them the glorious riches of this mystery"—Paul gestured to the group—"which is Christ in you."

Paul looked upward and launched his hands toward heaven. "The hope of glory!" *Colossians 1:27*

"The Son of God in us," I said. "That is earth-shattering news! Or at least it should be."

"And that is why we proclaim him," Paul said, "admonishing and teaching everyone in all wisdom to present every person perfect in Christ." *Colossians 1:28*

"Teaching and admonishing," I said. "Sounds like a great discipleship model. We're always looking for a good study guide for that."

2 Timothy 3:16

Paul looked down at my Bible. "All of Scripture is inspired by God and is profitable for teaching, for refuting error, for correction, and for training in righteousness"—

"If only people were more inclined to read it."

2 Timothy 3:17

—"so that those who serve God may be complete, fully equipped for every good work."

"And that's the aim of your discipleship, isn't it? To present people fully equipped— perfect in Christ."

Colossians 1:29

"That is the goal I labor and strive for," Paul said, "with God's power working in me."

"Good thing," I said, "because you sure couldn't do that in your own strength. I don't think anybody could."

Galatians 6:3

"If anyone thinks he is something when he is nothing," Paul shrugged, "he is deceived."

Philippians 2:7

"But Christ is something," I said. "Though he became nothing for our sake."

Ephesians 1:20–21
Philippians 2:9

"And that is why God raised him to the highest place!" Paul stood suddenly. "When God raised Christ from the dead, he sat him at his right hand on high. Exalting him above all rule and authority and"—Paul stabbed at the air, gouging out words to express the elevation of Christ—"and power. And dominion! Far above every name, whether of this age…or the age to come."

"Like I said, Christ is something."

Ephesians 1:22–23
Colossians 2:9

"And having placed everything under Christ's feet," Paul said, becoming very solemn, "God gave him to the church, as its supreme head. For the church is Christ's body—the fullness of him who fills all in all." Paul looked around the room. "For all the fullness of God resides in Christ."

Spiritual Blessings

Paul stood frozen, either in contemplation of those invincible truths or to allow time for them to sink in, then he sat down and spun back to me. He aimed two fingers straight at my heart.

"And you," he said, "by your union with Christ, you have been filled and are complete in him who is the head over all sovereignty and authority." *Colossians 2:10*

"I'm not sure all the saints know this," I said. "Sometimes I'm not even sure I know it."

Paul jumped up. "I know that Christ lives in me!" *Galatians 2:20*

"That's just what I mean, Paul." I waved toward him. "Know it personally, like you do."

"That was my prayer for the believers in Ephesus," Paul said, slowly sitting down again. "That Christ would dwell in their hearts through faith." *Ephesians 3:17*

"Yes," I said. "Dwell in their hearts."

Paul slipped into a faraway place. "And those in Galatia"—he slowly shook his head—"I suffered birth pains all over again until Christ would be formed in them." *Galatians 4:19*

"So obviously you want this for every believer," I said. "What happened in Galatia?"

"Oh, the foolish Galatians!" Paul said. "Some wanted to be back under the law." *Galatians 3:1; 4:21*

"Oh no, I hope this isn't—"

"I told them, 'If you allow yourselves to be circumcised, Christ will avail you nothing.'" *Galatians 5:2*

I knew it! I glanced around the room. Some people were rolling their eyes.

Paul caught it too. "Any of you who pursue righteousness through the law"—Paul banged the table—"you are separated from Christ." He slammed the table again. "And from grace." *Galatians 5:4*

"Paul, can we just move on here?" I raised my hands as in surrender. "This circumcision thing keeps getting you upset."

Galatians 5:1

"It was for our own freedom that Christ set us free!" Paul hammered the table again. He wasn't quite ready to move on. "Stand firm in it!" Another thump. "Do not be held again in slavery to the law."

I inched my chair back from the table.

Galatians 2:21

"If righteousness is through the law," Paul cried out, "then there was no need for Christ to die!"

Galatians 2:20

Paul started to stand up and then sat down again. "I have been crucified with Christ." He lowered his voice. "It is no longer I who live, but it is Jesus Christ who lives in me." His voice fell again. "And this life I live in the flesh…it is by faith in the Son of God, who loved me, and gave himself up for me."

I suddenly realized that I had stopped breathing. All I could manage was a weak, "…by faith."

No one moved or spoke.

"By faith," I said again. I took a deep breath. "But what about those who aren't sure of their faith? What would you say to someone like that?"

"Examine yourself to see whether you are in the faith," Paul said. "Test yourself."

"Well, yes," I said. "But how can you test yourself?"

2 Corinthians 13:5

"Do you not realize that Jesus Christ is in you?" Paul said. "Unless, of course, you fail the test."

"Fail the test?"

Romans 8:9

"Anyone who does not have the Spirit of Christ does not belong to Christ."

"Well, I know that Christ is in me," I said. "And I am in Christ." I looked over at Paul. "I just don't know it all the time."

2 Corinthians 1:21

"It is God who anoints us with the Holy Spirit and gives us security in Christ."

"That's good to know," I said. "The new me—secure in Christ."

"Again, it is of God that you are in Christ," said Paul, "who became our righteousness."

"Because we can't be righteous ourselves through the law."

"And our holiness," Paul said.

"Because we can never be good enough on our own."

"And our redemption," said Paul. — *1 Corinthians 1:30*

"Our salvation is only in Christ." I was glad to see things were picking up again.

"For in Jesus Christ neither circumcision nor uncircumcision profits anything," Paul said. "But a new creation is everything." — *Galatians 6:15*

"And it is everything, isn't it?" I said. "New and improved!"

"Created in God's likeness," Paul said, "in true righteousness and holiness." — *Ephesians 4:24*

"My old sin nature sloughed off like a snake skin!"

"A circumcision of the heart." Paul was smiling. "By the Spirit." — *Romans 2:29*

"No longer under the power of sin." I stood up.

Paul looked up at me. "Having been set free from sin." — *Romans 6:22*

"The Spirit of Christ is in me." I spun around.

"And through him—by faith—we enter into God's grace." Paul pushed his chair back. "And the hope of glory!" Paul was on his feet. — *Romans 5:2*

"Christ in me and me in Christ," I said. "His Spirit joined with mine." I spun again.

"Your life hidden with Christ." Paul was pacing back and forth. "In God himself!" — *Colossians 3:3*

"Hidden in glory!"

"You are a son and an heir of God through Christ." — *Galatians 4:7*

"I'm a child of—we all are children of God!" I couldn't stop skipping and turning.

"And if children, then heirs." Paul was beside me, moving as I moved. "Heirs of God and joint heirs with Christ." — *Romans 8:17*

"All my sins forgiven!" I sang it out. "They're gone—totally gone!"

"Peace with God through Christ," Paul said. — *Romans 5:1*

"Yes—yes! My heart at peace!"

<small>Titus 3:7</small>

"Made righteous by grace"—Paul was in lockstep now—"and heirs of eternal life."

"I can feel the righteousness—and the life!"

<small>Romans 8:1</small>

"There is no condemnation for those in Christ."

I stopped turning. "Paul, this is"—the room kept spinning—"it's all so real! How can people not believe this?"

<small>Romans 3:3</small>

"And what if some do not believe?" Paul said. "Will that cancel God's faithfulness? Never!"

"Well, I know it's true."

<small>Romans 3:4</small>

"Indeed," said Paul. "Let God be found true and every man a liar."

"True indeed." I had to sit down. "…every bit of it."

<small>Colossians 1:5</small>

Paul came back to the table and stood beside me. "All of which you heard before in the word of truth." He gently lifted my chin. "The gospel."

The room stopped spinning.

"A little embarrassing there," I said. "Dancing around like that."

<small>Romans 14:17</small>

"The kingdom of God is righteousness and peace…and joy in the Holy Spirit."

"I know—I felt it. It's all spiritual." I waved my hand. "Lots of blessings."

<small>Ephesians 1:3</small>

"Truly," said Paul. "God has blessed us on high with every spiritual blessing in Christ."

"On high?"

"In the heavenly places."

"How can we experience those blessings on 'low?" I asked. "Here in the earthly places?" It was more of a challenge than a question, and I saw a lot of heads nodding. "You were going to teach us that."

<small>Titus 1:1</small>

"That is why I was sent," Paul said, "for the faith of God's chosen people and the knowledge of the truth that produces godliness."

"Knowing what we are is a good start," I said, "but we need to know how to become what we are here in this world. How to live it out."

I looked up at Paul. He was looking at something I couldn't see. Something far beyond my horizon. And he was whispering things, "Love for all…hope laid up in heaven…bring forth fruit."

I was tired, but I made a mental note to explore that new territory with Paul. Tomorrow.

Colossians 1:4–6

5

Defeat Sin, Self and Satan

This is where the rubber meets the road. This is where the fruit of true repentance and sincere faith starts to pay off. This is where you can begin to apply all you know about the new creation—the new and improved you—to achieve victory over sin, self, and Satan.

Now if there is a victory, there must be a battle. And a battle there is! Satan is the enemy. Self is the willing collaborator. And sin is the fruit of that dark coalition.

Satan

Satan is real. And he is evil. And he leads a vast host of wicked demons. The Bible says the whole world is under his power. Jesus himself called Satan the ruler of this world.

Jesus was very specific about the devil. He said the devil was a murderer from the beginning. A murderer takes the life away from a person. Satan took spiritual life from Adam and Eve by lies and deceit—which resulted in their physical death—and he wants to do the same to you. Jesus said there is no truth in Satan, calling him a liar and the father of lies. And the Bible says Satan deceives the entire world.

The Bible also calls Satan the accuser, accusing Christians before God day and night. And he accuses us personally to make us feel guilty about sins God has already forgiven. Satan also tries to lead us into sin. The Bible calls the devil the tempter and describes how he even tempted Jesus to sin.

Self

During times of war, citizens of a country have been known to collaborate with an invading enemy to help overthrow the government. In our case, self is an all-too-willing collaborator with the enemy, Satan, who wants to destroy our spiritual life.

And self can get into enough trouble on its own, without Satan. If you doubt that, check out Chapter Two again. Still, you might be saying, "If it wasn't for Satan, I wouldn't be buried in all this trouble." But then someone might respond, "If it wasn't for your own self, maybe you wouldn't have gone there in the first place." The good news for believers is that the Holy Spirit has freed us from the power of sin and our old self.

In his Sermon on the Mount, Jesus set out a very high standard for how we need to live our lives. Many people say such a life is impossible, but the fact is Jesus came to earth so that we can actually live like that!

Sin

Sadly, sin and its destructive forces have plagued mankind since the fall of Adam and Eve in the Garden of Eden. And yet the ultimate problem with sin is that it separates us from a holy God.

But the incredibly good news is that God sent Jesus to put away sin once and for all by his sacrificial death on the cross. And the Bible says if we confess our sins, God will forgive our sins and cleanse us from all unrighteousness. Thus, we can have a living relationship with God from that moment on—and forever.

In all of this, the forgiveness of sin, your new creation, and the overcoming life, God's plan continues to unfold. And as history moves toward its end, these are all part of something bigger, grander, and greater than we could ever imagine. In the meantime, we need to learn how to work with this new life in us—for it is the life and power of God himself.

What does it take to walk and live in this spiritual realm of mind-boggling power to overcome sin, self, and Satan?

I knew Paul could tell us that.

CHRIST THE KEY

"Paul, let's keep this simple. What's the secret of defeating sin and self and—"

"Our battle is not against flesh and blood…"

"OK, not so simple."

"But against principalities."

"Excuse me?"

"Our battle is against powers."

"What kind of powers?"

"The rulers of this darkness."

"Could you just be a little more specific, Paul?"

Ephesians 6:12 — "Against the cosmic powers and unseen spiritual forces of evil and wickedness in the heavenly realms."

"Uh oh. We're dead."

2 Corinthians 10:7 — Paul smiled. "You look at the outward appearance of things."

"What do you mean?"

Colossians 2:15 — "God has disarmed the principalities and powers," Paul said. "He even made a show of them, triumphing over them in the cross."

"Disarmed them all…" I said. "Just not sure how he—"

Colossians 2:13–14 — "God forgave us all our sins, wiping out the handwriting against us with its decrees opposing us." Paul turned to the group and waved a hand of dismissal. "He has taken it away once for all, having nailed it to the cross."

"So no more ammunition for the bad guys!" I said. "Our sins gone. The law taken away. But do you suppose that means we can do whatever we want?"

Romans 3:8; 6:15 — "What then?" Paul twisted round to face me. "Are we to sin because we are under grace and no longer under the law? May it never be! Why not say—as some falsely accuse me of saying—'Let us do evil that good may come.' Their condemnation is deserved!"

Paul was turning several shades of red. "Sin no longer has power over you! For you are not living under the law but under grace! Do you not remember me telling you these things?" *2 Thessalonians 2:5*
Romans 6:14

How soon we forget. "I'm sorry Paul. As I think about it, the Bible does say Jesus came to undo the works of the devil. So, if grace can somehow free us from his grip…" I clenched my jaw. "But I'd say Satan is still quite active." *1 John 3:8*

"I myself received a thorn in the flesh," said Paul. "A messenger of Satan to buffet me." *2 Corinthians 12:7*

"See? He still torments us," I said. "Him and his demons. And he still deceives people."

"And no wonder!" Paul said. "For even Satan disguises himself as an angel of light." *2 Corinthians 11:14*

"So we're back to where we started," I said. "How do we fight Satan and his evil spirits?"

"You don't."

"Paul, I was hoping to keep this simple." I nodded toward the group. "For all of us."

"We who boast in Jesus Christ," said Paul, "do not trust in the flesh." *Philippians 3:3*

"Well, it's my flesh that's in this world," I said, "and that's how I fight my battles."

"Why," Paul said, "if you died with Christ to the ways of the world, do you act as though you still live in the world—submitting to its rules?" *Colossians 2:20*

"Rules tell us what to do," I said. "And what not to do."

"Do not touch! Do not eat! Do not—" Paul shrugged and shook his head in disgust. "Christ did away with the law…its commandments and ordinances." *Colossians 2:21*
Ephesians 2:15

"We need some kind of guidelines!"

Paul planted his elbows on the table and buried his face in his hands. "You follow mere human directions and instructions." *Colossians 2:22*

"Yes, of how to live our lives."

Defeat Sin, Self and Satan

Colossians 2:23	"Such rules do have a reputation of wisdom in self-made religion…and humility and hard treatment of the body." Paul lifted his head to look at me. "But they are useless against the indulgence of the flesh."
	"OK, so maybe not in our own strength," I said.
Colossians 2:8	Paul turned to the room. "Be careful that no one leads you astray according to human traditions and the principles of this world." Paul swiveled back and looked me square in the eye. "And not in accordance with Christ."
	"Why do you say that? To me?"
2 Corinthians 11:3	"I fear that just as Satan deceived Eve by his craftiness, you may be led astray from the simplicity and purity that is in Christ."
	"Are you saying our battle plan can be reduced to one word? Christ?"
1 Corinthians 2:1–2	"It was not with mere words of eloquence or cleverness that I proclaimed the mystery of God." Paul turned back to the group. "For I had determined to know nothing among you but Jesus Christ—and him crucified."
	"Well, you can't get any simpler than that," I said. "But how do you live that out?"
Galatians 2:20	"I said it before. I live my life by faith in the Son of God who gave himself for me."
	"There has to be more to it than that."
	"You still look at the surface of things," Paul said. "For although we walk in the flesh, we do not wage war according to the flesh." He smiled as though sheltering a treasured secret.
	"So how do you wage war?"
2 Corinthians 10:3–4, 7	"The weapons of our warfare are not of the flesh—but have divine power."
	I shook my head. "That didn't really answer—"
2 Corinthians 6:7	"In all things we show ourselves as God's servants with the weapons of righteousness." Paul looked down at his hands, then up at me. "By the word of truth. In the power of God."
	"The word of truth?"

"The gospel of Christ."

"In the power of God?"

"The gospel of Christ is…the power of God." *Romans 1:16*

"And that brings us back to Christ again," I said, making a large circle with my finger. "And you do this in all things—all the time?"

"Yes, in many an hour of endurance," Paul said. "In troubles, in hardships, in difficulties, in floggings, in imprisonments, in riots, in toils, in sleepless nights, in hunger—" *2 Corinthians 6:4–5*

"Well then," I said, "it should work for us—in our daily trials."

"For God has delivered us from the powers of darkness," said Paul, "and brought us into the kingdom of his beloved Son." *Colossians 1:13*

"The spiritual realm of God," I said. "And his power."

Paul turned to the room. "For although you were once darkness, you are now light in the Lord." Paul slowly walked his fingers across the table. "Therefore walk as children of the light." He walked his fingers back to himself. "Discerning what is pleasing to the Lord." *Ephesians 5:8, 10*

The room went silent. I was flattered that Paul had copied my finger-walking technique—I thought it had worked quite well for him. A few people started talking quietly with one another.

Paul stood and raised his voice. "If you live for the flesh, you will certainly die!" He had never looked or sounded more serious. "But if you put to death the deeds of the body by the power of the Spirit"—Paul placed both hands on his heart—"you will live!" *Romans 8:13*

"Can you teach us how to do that?" I asked, glancing around the room. I saw a few heads nodding and one huge, hopeful smile in the corner.

I looked up at Paul. He was lost in thought. Everyone stayed quite still, giving him time to sift through the memories.

Paul slowly sat down in his chair. "God has made us alive," he said, "together with Christ." *Ephesians 2:5*

"Spiritually alive."

"Yes, and if we live by the Spirit, let us also walk by the Spirit." Paul started to rock slightly in his chair. "Taking no thought for the desires of the flesh—to gratify them."

Galatians 5:25
Romans 13:14

"Do you mean, like, not even think about it?"

Paul was rocking slowly, side to side. "For the desires of the flesh are contrary to the Spirit. And the desires of the Spirit against the flesh. They oppose each other"—Paul brought his two fists together—"so you cannot do what you wish."

Galatians 5:17

"Right there!" I said. "Right there! You nailed our number one problem." There was a sharp murmur of assent in the room. "So what's the solution?"

"I just said it."

"We just missed it."

"I say then…" Paul leaned out toward the group. "Walk by the Spirit"—people strained forward to hear—"and you will not gratify the desires of the flesh."

Galatians 5:16

Spiritual Weapons

Everyone leaned back again. The smile in the corner disappeared. "So, if we are able to do this at all," I said helpfully, "it will be only by having God's Spirit in us."

"Yes," said Paul, "with God's Spirit himself bearing the fruit—in every form of goodness and righteousness and truth."

Ephesians 5:9

"I bet they call it fruit because it comes naturally by the Spirit," I said. "Like a fruit tree produces an apple or an orange."

"But the fruit produced by the Spirit"—Paul reached out his hand as though plucking something—"is love, joy, peace, patience, kindness, goodness, faith, gentleness, self-control—"

Galatians 5:22–23

"The hidden plan!" I snatched up my Bible. "God promised to put his Spirit in us so we would walk in his laws and keep his decrees."

Ezekiel 36:27

"And now set free from the law," said Paul, "we can serve God in the newness of the Spirit and not the old way of the written law."

Romans 7:6

"Keeping the law without the law!" I said. "Now I see why you get so upset about circumcision. It's a step back into the bondage of the law!"

"Knowing this," said Paul, "that the law is not given for the righteous but for the lawless and unruly, for the ungodly and wicked, for the unholy and godless, for those who abuse their fathers or mothers, for murderers—" *1 Timothy 1:9*

"What was it you said? Now we can serve in the newness of the Spirit? I liked the sound of that."

"If you are led by the Spirit"—Paul swatted at a fly—"you are not under the law." *Galatians 5:18*

"We want to know how to serve in newness of the Spirit!" That sparked more nodding.

"You must put on the Lord Jesus Christ." *Romans 13:14*

"You just said to be led by the Spirit."

"But the Lord is the Spirit!" Paul threw up his hands. "And where the Spirit of the Lord is—there is the freedom." *2 Corinthians 3:17*

"So to put on Christ is to have his Spirit in us, leading us," I said. "Jesus told his disciples that those who abide in him—and him in them—will bear fruit. A lot of fruit." *John 15:5*

"You must clothe yourselves in that new self," Paul said, "created according to God in true righteousness and holiness." *Ephesians 4:24*

"Then we need to wrap ourselves in this new life—bundle ourselves up in it—with every thought we have and choice we make! So his power will enable us to walk in freedom from sin."

"And you must put off your former ways of the old self," said Paul, "which is corrupted by deceitful desires." *Ephesians 4:22*

"It's only the new self that can live to please God," I said, "because our new self has the same nature and power as Jesus."

"As I said, I have been crucified with Christ, and it is no longer I who live—but it is Christ who lives in me." *Galatians 2:20*

"May that be true for all of us!"

Romans 7:4	"And so it is," Paul said, looking around the room. "You died to the law in the body of Christ that you might be united to him who was raised from the dead. To bear fruit to God."

"Yes, bear fruit to God," I said. "But I did want to keep it simple."

"How did you receive the Lord Jesus Christ?"

"I turned from sin and trusted in his death for me."

Colossians 2:6 — "So then," said Paul, "just as you received Christ, so walk in him."

"You mean I should turn from sin and trust in Christ…like, all the time?"

Colossians 2:7 — "Yes, solidly rooted and being built up in him," Paul said, "firm in the faith just as you were taught it. Overflowing with faith and giving thanks to God."

"Well, you can't make it any simpler than that!"

Ephesians 5:18 — Paul looked out the window, and I followed his line of sight just in time to see a burst of pigeons launch from the courtyard. Paul turned back to me. "You must be filled with the Spirit."

"I guess that makes sense," I said, "if we want to live and walk in the Spirit."

Ephesians 4:30 — "Do not grieve God's Holy Spirit," said Paul. "For it was by that Spirit God sealed you as his for the day of redemption."

"Grieve the Spirit?"

1 Thessalonians 5:19 — "Do not quench the Spirit."

"And who would want to do that?" I waved a hand. "Our only source of power!"

Ephesians 4:31 — "Then you must put away all anger, rage, malice, slander, and filthy talk."

Ephesians 4:28 / Colossians 3:9 — "And likely anything else that's wrong," I said. "Lying, stealing—"

"Do not give the devil an opening."

"Keep the Spirit in and Satan out," I said. "Sounds simple, but—"

Ephesians 4:26 / 2 Corinthians 2:11 — "If you become angry, do not sin," Paul said. "Do not let the sun go down on your anger, in case Satan should take advantage of you. For we are not unaware of his evil schemes."

"I know I've said some angry things—thinking about stuff long after the sun went down!"

"You must not give the devil an opportunity!" said Paul. "Never let any foul word pass your lips, but only such good words as the occasion demands, that they may impart grace to those who hear them." — *Ephesians 4:27, 29*

"James, the brother of Jesus, called the tongue a restless evil, filled with deadly poison!" I pressed my tongue against my teeth. "He said anyone who can control the tongue is perfect and can control the whole body as well." — *James 3:2, 8*

"One day every tongue will declare that Jesus Christ is Lord," said Paul, "to the glory of God the Father." — *Philippians 2:11*

"And in the meantime, maybe we should focus on our tongue—get mastery there!"

"For Scripture says that every knee will bend before the Lord, and every tongue will praise God." — *Romans 14:11*

"If we can control our tongue," I said, "we should be able to control our whole body. Working out our salvation—from the inside out!"

"Having put on the new self," said Paul, "which is being renewed in knowledge after the image of its creator." — *Colossians 3:10*

"Becoming what we are!" I turned to Paul. "So how do we do that again?"

Paul tapped his head. "The spirit of your minds must be constantly renewed." — *Ephesians 4:23*

"Yeah, I know." I nodded. "Our minds can get us into a lot of trouble."

"Because the mind set on the flesh is hostile to God," Paul said. "It does not submit to the law of God." Paul shrugged. "Actually, it cannot." — *Romans 8:7*

"Cannot?"

Paul frowned and slowly shook his head as one who had tried it. "Those in the flesh are not able to please God. For those living — *Romans 8:8* according to the flesh have set their minds on the things of the flesh."

"A nasty business."

Romans 8:5 "But those living according to the Spirit have set their minds on the things of the Spirit."

"So it's all about where we focus our minds," I said. "The results we get."

Romans 8:6 "The mind set on the flesh brings forth death," said Paul. "But the mind set on the Spirit yields life and peace."

"Death or life," I said. "Sounds like a no brainer."

1 Thessalonians 5:5
Romans 13:12 Paul shot a quick glance at me before turning to those around us. "Indeed, for all you who are in Christ are sons of the light and of the day. We do not belong to the night or to darkness. Therefore, let us throw off the deeds of darkness and put on the armor of light."

"The armor of light?"

1 Thessalonians 5:8–9 "Yes. Let us who belong to the day control ourselves, putting on the hope of salvation as a helmet." Paul mimicked putting on a helmet. "For God did not appoint us to wrath, but to obtain salvation through Jesus Christ."

A Gospel Mind

Destined for salvation! That was a well-timed observation of Paul, and people seemed to want to settle into that thought. They were nodding and turning to one another as Paul called them back.

Ephesians 6:10 "My friends!" said Paul. "From this moment on, you must be strong in the Lord and in the power that comes from him."

"The trick is to keep that power working in us," I said. "Specially when Satan tempts us."

Ephesians 6:11 "You must put on the full armor of God if you are to stand against the plots and schemes of the devil."

"Ah, yes, the armor of light," I said. "You told us to put on a helmet."

"I did," said Paul. "Take up the helmet of salvation, for God set his seal upon us and gave us his Spirit in our hearts as a pledge." *2 Corinthians 1:22*

"Our guarantee of salvation when Christ returns!"

"Stand your ground then, with that word of truth for your belt and with righteousness for your breastplate." *Ephesians 6:14*

"Armed with the good news of the gospel and the righteousness of God himself," I said. "Through faith in Jesus." *Romans 3:22*

"Prepare your feet with the readiness and eagerness given by the gospel of peace." Paul tapped his chest. "And let this peace of God control your hearts. Always thanking God." *Ephesians 6:15 / Colossians 3:15*

"It'd be pretty hard to disturb a heart at peace with God and overflowing with thankfulness. That's clever, Paul, because if we're always thanking God we'll always be mindful of that peace."

"And in every situation," Paul said, smiling, "take up the shield of faith. For with it you will be able to extinguish all the flaming arrows of the evil one." *Ephesians 6:16*

"And that's faith in…Jesus Christ, right?"

"Through whom we have found deliverance in the forgiveness of sins." *Colossians 1:14*

"Everything keeps coming back to Christ, doesn't it?"

"And take hold of the sword of—"

"A sword!" I cried. "At last, a weapon!"

"The sword of the Spirit," Paul said, "which is the word of God." *Ephesians 6:17*

"I know God's word is powerful," I said. "It speaks to my soul—as though it's alive."

"Because the gospel did not come to you in word only, but also with power in the Holy Spirit." *1 Thessalonians 1:5*

"So, when I first heard the gospel…like, really heard it—"

"You accepted it," Paul said, "not as the word of man, but as it truly is—the word of God." Paul looked around the room. "Which even now is doing its work in you who believe." *1 Thessalonians 2:13*

"So all this talk about putting on the spiritual armor of God—it's really about putting on the gospel. And the gospel is all about

Christ." I turned to Paul. "I see why you resolved to know nothing but Jesus Christ and him crucified!"

Romans 1:16

"The gospel of Christ is the power of God unto salvation—for everyone who believes."

"Then we better develop a gospel mind," I said, "thinking about what Christ did for us. Which is a lot to think about."

"Yes, and beyond that, my friends," Paul said, "whatever things are true, and whatever is honorable—"

"Now just a minute, Paul…"

"Whatever is righteous, whatever is pure—"

"This isn't just some feel good…"

"Whatever is admirable, whatever is noble—"

"Positive thinking trick, is it?"

Philippians 4:8

"If there is any virtue or anything worthy of praise," Paul continued, his eyes fastening on mine, "think on these things."

We slipped into another staring spell where Paul waited for me to catch up to him. And as we stared at each other, I had the unsettling sense that a few others were waiting too.

"OK, I think I get it!" I said. "This is how you want us to move toward holiness in everything we say and do."

Philippians 4:9

"Moreover," said Paul, turning to the room, "if you put into practice what you learned, and all that you heard me say and saw me do, the God of peace will be with you."

"Because thought precedes action," I said, as the simple truth dawned on me.

"So be transformed by the renewing of your mind," said Paul. "And do not be conformed to the fashion of this world."

"Right thoughts, right actions," I added. We were working in true tandem now.

Romans 12:2
Colossians 3:1

"That you may test and prove the good and perfect will of God." Paul turned once more toward the group. "Since you were raised to life with Christ, strive after things that are above, where Christ is seated at the right hand of God."

"Heavenly things," I said.

"Yes, set your minds upon the things that are above, not upon the things of earth." *Colossians 3:2*

"Is this one of your faith secrets, Paul? How you got through all your ordeals?"

"We do not look to what is seen, but to that which is unseen." A wave of emotions surged across Paul's eyes. "For what is seen is temporary, but what is unseen is eternal." *2 Corinthians 4:18*

"The earthly versus the heavenly."

"And the sufferings of this life are not comparable with the glory to be revealed in us." *Romans 8:18*

"Our sufferings," I said. "That's all we can think about when we're up to our necks in alligators. Easy to lose sight of the goal." *2 Corinthians 5:7*

"We walk by faith—not by sight."

"By faith…in?"

"The hope of eternal life," said Paul, "which God promised before time." *Titus 1:2*

"And not by sight."

"Who hopes for what he can see?" Paul said. "But when we hope for what is unseen, we look for it with patient endurance." *Romans 8:25*

"And you're looking for…?"

"The blessed hope!" said Paul. "The appearing in glory of our great God and Savior, Jesus Christ!" *Titus 2:13*

Paul stood suddenly and waved his hand across the room. "And for our full adoption as sons—the redemption of our bodies!" Paul's hands shot skyward. "Raised up in glory!" *Romans 8:23* \
1 Corinthians 15:43

"I'm feeling a little swamped here, Paul." I looked around and saw some heads nodding. "Maybe just give us some simple thing to help us on our journey to glory. One thing, perhaps…that you do?"

"My friends," Paul said, lowering his head and dropping his hands. "I do not regard myself as having yet laid hold of it. But there is one thing I do."

Paul threw an imaginary load off his back and raised his eyes upward. "This one thing! Forgetting what lies behind and straining for what lies ahead, I press on to gain the prize of the upward call God gave me in Jesus Christ."

Philippians 3:13–14

"Forget the past," I said, "and press ahead to the future." One simple thing, indeed. But I still felt overwhelmed, and I knew I wasn't the only one. "Paul, would you pray for us?"

In an instant, Paul fell to his knees. "For this reason, I kneel before the Father. And I pray you will be strengthened with power through his Spirit in your inmost soul…so that Christ may make his home within your hearts through faith."

"Maybe pray for all believers too, Paul."

Ephesians 3:14, 16–19

"And I pray that you, firmly rooted and established in love, may with all Christ's people be able to perceive the width and length and height and depth…and to know the love of Christ, and so be filled with God himself."

The room was still. Paul heaved a ragged sigh and shifted his weight.

Ephesians 3:20–21

"Now to him who is able to do more than we can ask or imagine by his power working in us—to him be all glory through the church and through Jesus Christ, for all generations, forever and ever. Amen."

More silence.

"Amen, indeed," I said. "And thank you, Paul."

The only sound was a soft rustling as people stirred and started to leave.

I helped Paul back to his feet. "So the same power we can live by now will also raise us up from death. Can't wait to talk about that!"

6

THE PRIZE— ETERNAL LIFE

Everlasting life—ah, yes, what a vision!

People have dreamed of eternal life as long as they have been on earth. A good example is a man named Ponce de Leon. He was a Spanish explorer, and in 1513 was the first European to set foot on what is now Florida. Meeting with the local native leaders, he heard of a remarkable Fountain of Youth. History tells us that the Spaniards searched every river, stream, lagoon, and pond along the Florida coast looking for the legendary fountain. And even though they never found it, they never stopped believing in it.

On the other hand, there are those who see eternal life as just a pipe dream—an airy-fairy kind of fantasy. The apostle Paul encountered this when he preached the gospel in Athens. The Bible tells us the Athenians and the foreigners staying in the city spent all their time discussing the latest new thing. But when the philosophers and other scholars heard Paul speak about the resurrection of the dead, they mocked him and laughed in contempt. We see this same denial and contemptuous scoffing at God's truth among many scientists and philosophers today.

Albert Einstein, the genius who gave the world $E=mc^2$, stated flatly, "I do not believe in the immortality of the individual." (*Albert Einstein, The Human Side: Glimpses from His Archives*)

Thomas Edison said, "Human beings, individually, cannot be immortal, as I see it…for they are mere aggregates of cells." (*The Columbian Magazine*)

Mark Twain quipped, "One of the proofs of the immortality of the soul is that myriads have believed it. They also believed the world was flat." (*Goodreads*)

Quite apart from what these and other respected thinkers and authors say about it, the fact is that eternal life—immortality—is very real. The resurrection of Jesus Christ settled that debate nearly two millennia ago. Ever since then, people have either been denying it or looking for it in all the wrong places, such as through science or along the coast of Florida.

Little do they know that God had a secret. A secret so secret he kept it hidden for ages and generations—until Jesus Christ came, as the prophets said he would, to reveal things that were "kept secret from the foundation of the world." Jesus told his disciples that many wise men and kings had longed to know these things—and they never did. But now the secret is out!

Imagine a day when the sun will rise over the earth's horizon for the very last time. Can you? That day is what the Bible calls "the last day." Jesus said, "Everyone who believes in me will receive everlasting life, and I will raise him up at the last day."

We call it the gospel. It is the great news of God's salvation of mankind. Mind you, some people can become quite upset at hearing that news because, as it turns out, the gospel has a pretty serious downside too.

I picked that up right away in my conversation with Paul.

A Prophet Speaks

Everybody was just sitting there looking at one another until I broke the silence. "Well, you sure got their attention with that last comment, Paul."

"All I said was God is doing something they'll never believe." Paul looked around slowly. "Even if I tell them about it."

"Actually," I said, "I think it was that other part—something about a prophet's threat."

"It was a warning."

"What was that all about?"

"From a gospel message I gave in Antioch." Acts 13:14, 26

"Antioch?"

"Yes, in a synagogue," Paul said. "I talked about our history as Jews, how our leaders failed to recognize Jesus as the promised Messiah, and how they had him executed and laid in a tomb." Acts 13:27, 29

"They thought they were done with him."

"But God raised him from the dead." Acts 13:30

"A lot of people don't believe that."

"A lot of people saw him," Paul said. "For a lot of days." Acts 13:31

"How'd they know it was him?" I mused aloud.

"They had come to Jerusalem with him."

"I'm just saying what a lot of people think, Paul. Let's get back to your message in Antioch."

"I told them God had fulfilled the promise he made to our ancestors by raising Jesus from the dead." Acts 13:32–33

"The promised resurrection."

"And therefore I was proclaiming the forgiveness of all our sins through Jesus—for everyone who believes." Acts 13:38–39

"And how was all that received?"

"The Gentiles were glad and celebrated the good news." Acts 13:48

"That's great!" I said. "Get the gospel to the non-Jews."

"But the Jews rejected it outright. They stirred up trouble and had us kicked out of town." Paul's face hardened. "But I warned them. I said to watch out that what the prophet said does not come true of them—" Acts 13:40, 50

"Yes, the prophet's threat," I said. "What was that again?"

"Habakkuk's warning."

"Ah, Habakkuk," I said. "I always had trouble spelling that."

"God revealed his gospel through him," said Paul, "as through all his prophets in the holy Scriptures." Romans 1:2, 17

The Prize—Eternal Life

"Yes, I know. He said the righteous will live by faith. But I don't remember him saying—"

Habakkuk 2:4

"Look, you scoffers, and wonder and marvel…and perish!" For the briefest moment, Paul was the prophet. "For I am doing a work in your days which you will not believe, even if you were told about it."

Acts 13:41

"That's the part," I said. "About the scoffers perishing. That's what got a few of us here sitting up straight."

"I simply told them to watch out." Paul wagged his finger. "For the prophet said those who despise and deny this new work of God will surely perish."

"You know, Paul, people today aren't really open to that kind of talk."

"They never were."

"So we soft-pedal that part a bit. And try to make the message more, ah…appealing."

"You have to tell people God's truth," Paul countered. "All of it."

"I'm not disputing that." I shifted in my chair. "It's just that I was hoping to start this off on more of a positive note."

2 Corinthians 6:1–2
1 Corinthians 7:29

"Listen," Paul said. "Now is the time of God's favor. I'm telling you—today is the day of salvation. And the time is short. So do not despise God's grace."

"You know I don't despise God's grace, Paul. In fact, I'd prefer to talk about that."

2 Timothy 4:3

"I knew a time would come when people would not tolerate sound teaching." Paul shook his head. "That they would follow their own desires and surround themselves with teachers who say what their itching ears want to hear."

"Well yes, we do have some of that going on, but—"

2 Timothy 4:4

"And turn their ears away from the truth," Paul continued, "and give their attention to foolish myths instead."

"Oh no! It's not that!" I said. "It's just that God's gospel has so many lovely facets. Bright and beautiful—like a finely cut diamond. People like to hear about those things."

"I am not ashamed of the gospel." Paul turned to look at me, his eyes sharp and hard. "And you also must do your utmost to show yourself true to God, a workman with no reason to be ashamed, accurately handling the word of truth." *Romans 1:16 / 2 Timothy 2:15*

"Of course," I said. "But earlier you called it the good news of our salvation. And Luke, who traveled with you, he called it the message of God's grace." *Acts 14:3*

"Yes, the message of his grace…" Paul's eyes softened. "Which can give you an inheritance among all those—" *Acts 20:32*

"The inheritance! That's eternal life, right? The new thing God was doing. The gospel."

"It is indeed." Paul looked at the group. "For I brought you that same gospel which I also received. That Christ died for our sins as the Scriptures foretold. That he was buried, and on the third day he was raised up—" *1 Corinthians 15:3–4*

"Still, a lot of people say there is no resurrection. Even some here, I think."

Paul's face flushed. "If our hope in Christ is only for this life, we of all people are the most to be pitied." He slowly surveyed the group. "How is it that some of you say there is no resurrection of the dead?" *1 Corinthians 15:12, 19*

"I don't want to make trouble…"

"If Christ has not been raised, our preaching is in vain and your faith is useless!" *1 Corinthians 15:14*

"Paul, I—"

"For if there is no resurrection of the dead, then even Christ has not been raised." Paul's eyes flashed fire across the room. "And if Christ has not been raised, again I say your faith is worthless. You all are still in your sins!" *1 Corinthians 15:16–17*

"That's right," I chimed in, "even Jesus himself said he would rise from the dead." *Mark 9:31*

Paul stood up, catching his leg on the chair. "And we also testified that God has raised up Christ." *1 Corinthians 15:15*

1 Corinthians 15:5–7

Paul started counting with his fingers. "And he was seen by Peter and then the twelve." Paul soon ran out of fingers and waved his arms wide. "Afterward he was seen by more than five hundred at one time. After that, he appeared to James, then all the apostles."

1 Corinthians 15:8

Paul half-fell back into his chair. "Last of all, he appeared even to me—as to one abnormally born into the family of apostles."

Christ's Return

1 Corinthians 15:20

Paul had the uncanny ability to turn a room as silent as stone. Nobody moved. Paul straightened up and looked hard at me. "The fact is Christ has been raised from the dead—the first-fruits of those who sleep."

"Paul, you know I believe this."

2 Timothy 2:8

"You do," said Paul. "And you must never forget it. Jesus Christ, a descendant of David, was raised up from the dead."

"Yes, Jesus, fully man—raised from the dead." Paul sure could heat up fast, but he cooled down quickly too.

Romans 6:9

"And knowing that Christ was raised from the dead," Paul said, "we know he will never die again. Death no longer has power over him."

"But why must we never forget his resurrection?"

2 Corinthians 4:14

"Because we know that he who raised the Lord Jesus will raise us also and will bring us into his presence."

"Yes, of course!" I said. "Knowing we'll die one day, that is good news to hang on to!"

Romans 6:23
1 Corinthians 15:22-23

"The gift of God is life and immortality in Jesus Christ our Lord," Paul said, "for just as in Adam all die, in Christ all will be made alive." Paul lifted a finger in caution. "But each in order—Christ the first-fruits, and then, at his coming, those who belong to Christ."

"With Christ now raised," I said, "one day God will raise us up. His sons and daughters!"

"Nature will also be set free from its bondage to decay into the glorious freedom of the children of God." *Romans 8:21*

"Yes! The birth of the new heavens and earth," I said. "Not like this fallen, sinful world." Paul and I were in harmony again.

"For all creation was subjected to imperfection"—Paul turned to the group and smiled—"yet with hope that someday…" Paul drifted off into a contemplation of eternity, it seemed. *Romans 8:20*

"God talked about that hope through his prophets," I said, opening my Bible. "Listen to this from Isaiah. 'Behold! I will create new heavens and a new earth—and the former things will not be remembered at all. Be glad and rejoice forever in that which I will create.'" *Isaiah 65:17–18*

"Everything that was written in those earlier times"—Paul was back—"was written so we might have hope through the encouragement drawn from the Scriptures." *Romans 15:4*

"And the apostle John's revelation from heaven was written to encourage us too!" I turned to the last page of my Bible and read, "I heard a loud voice from heaven say, 'There will be no more death. Nor mourning, nor crying. Nor any more pain. For the old order has passed away.' And the one seated on the throne said, 'Behold, I am making all things new!'" *Revelation 21:3–5*

"Yes," said Paul, "and may God fill you with joy and peace in believing this, so you may overflow with hope in the power of the Holy Spirit." *Romans 15:13*

"See!" I said. "All these lovely gospel truths! Salvation. Eternal life. They give us hope."

"More than hope, for as surely as God has raised the Lord, in the same way he will raise us up also." Paul looked slowly around the room. "Those who believe what we preached." *1 Corinthians 1:21; 6:14*

"And for those who don't believe? Is that the Habakkuk threat, Paul?"

"When the Lord Jesus is revealed from heaven in flaming fire with his mighty angels, he will inflict punishment upon those who do not know God." Paul's eyes narrowed and his voice *2 Thessalonians 1:7–8* hardened. "And on those who do not submit to the gospel of Christ."

"What kind of punishment?" It was out before I knew it. Like a lot of my questions.

2 Thessalonians 1:9

"They will be punished with eternal misery—banished forever from the presence of the Lord and the glorious display of his power."

"That does seem harsh," I said. "Judgment hurtling down on them—and the loss of an eternity of blessing. I just wonder if we couldn't be a little more subtle."

Acts 20:20

"I never held back from declaring anything that could be profitable for one's good."

"You know, Paul? I think I'm starting to see the importance of doing that."

1 Corinthians 3:18

"Let no one be deceived." Paul turned to those listening. "If someone among you thinks he is wise in this world, let him become a fool that he may become wise."

"Yes," I said, "and receive the gift of eternal life." I loved helping Paul.

1 Corinthians 3:19

"For in God's sight," said Paul, "the wisdom of this world is foolishness."

"I know people who think that the gospel, the cross—it's all foolishness. They make jokes."

1 Corinthians 1:18, 24

"The message of the cross is foolishness to those on the path to destruction," Paul said. "But to those who are called, Christ is the power of God and the wisdom of God."

"How strange," I said, "that the world's wisdom is foolishness to God, and God's wisdom is foolishness to the world. Something's wrong with that picture."

1 Corinthians 1:20

"Where is the wise? Where is the scholar? The learned debater of this age?" Paul waved his hand in the air, taking in all of Rome. Or the world. "Has not God made the wisdom of this world foolish?"

People in the room were starting to fidget, but I could tell that Paul was just getting warmed up.

"And since the world did not come to know God through its own wisdom, God was pleased through the foolishness of our gospel message to save those who believe." *1 Corinthians 1:21*

A man and a woman stood and gathered up some small bags.

"Yet there is a wisdom that we speak among the mature," Paul said. "But it is not the wisdom of this world." *1 Corinthians 2:6*

They started toward the door and then slowed, looking back.

"Rather, we teach the wisdom of God." Paul glanced at them and kept going. "The hidden plan God determined before time began. A plan for our glory." *1 Corinthians 2:7*

"Maybe we should jump into that teaching." I smiled at the deserting couple. "What's that about glory, Paul?"

Paul smiled broadly. "We boast in our hope of sharing the glory of God." *Romans 5:2*

"God's going to share his glory with us," I said, with one eye on the couple. "What a day that will be!"

"On that day," Paul said, "when Christ comes to be glorified in his holy ones and honored among all those who believed." *2 Thessalonians 1:10*

"Let's talk about that day." Out of the corner of my eye, I caught the wandering couple heading back toward their bench. "Our resurrection day!"

"But someone may ask, 'How do the dead rise?'" Paul said. "'And in what body will they come?'" *1 Corinthians 15:35*

"OK, I'll ask that," I said.

"When you sow a seed," Paul said, "you do not sow the body that will be, but a mere grain—say, of wheat or something else." Paul pointed upward. "God gives it the body he pleases. To each seed its special body." *1 Corinthians 15:37–38*

"That sure works for wheat," I said, "but what about people?"

"It is the same with the resurrection of the dead," Paul said. "It is sown a perishable body—but it is raised imperishable." *1 Corinthians 15:42*

The Prize—Eternal Life

"Never again to die or decay."

"It is sown in shame—but it is raised in glory."

"The glory of Christ himself."

1 Corinthians 15:43

"Sown in weakness"—Paul dropped his hand, clenched it, and lifted up a fist—"it is raised in power!"

"Our dead body raised imperishable," I said, "in glory and in power! That sounds like Christ's resurrected body!"

Philippians 3:21

"His body indeed," said Paul. "For Christ, by his ability to make everything subject to himself, will make our lowly body to be like his glorious body!" Paul was positively glowing.

Our New Body

I quickly checked the room. There were still a few skeptics. "Paul, that would be quite a makeover. Can you just talk a little more about that?"

1 Corinthians 15:44

"It is sown a natural body," said Paul with a quick shrug, "it is raised a spiritual body."

"I know my physical body…but a spiritual body?"

1 Corinthians 15:45

"Just as Adam, the first man, was made a living soul, the last Adam became a life-giving spirit."

We still weren't following. Paul must have read a few faces, because he slowed it down. "The first man was of the earth."

Genesis 2:7

"Adam," I said. "God made him from the dust of the ground."

"And as was the man of dust, so also are all those of the dust."

"Yes, we all are like the first Adam," I said. "We are all his descendants."

1 Corinthians 15:47

"The second man is from heaven."

"Jesus," I said. "The Son of God."

1 Corinthians 15:48

Paul was keeping it nice and slow. "And as is the man of heaven, so also are all those of heaven."

"Those who are born again," I said, nodding my head. "Born of God."

"And if there is a natural body"—Paul motioned toward the group with both hands—"there is also a spiritual body." He pointed upward. "And just as we now bear the image of the man of dust," Paul added, "we then will bear the image of the man of heaven."

1 Corinthians 15:49

"When Jesus comes back, right, Paul?"

"Yes, when Christ who is our life appears, then we also will appear with him in glory."

Colossians 3:4

"We'll rise up right out of our graves," I said. "Just like Jesus did."

"That is true," said Paul. "If the Spirit of him who raised Jesus from the dead lives within you, he will also give life to your mortal bodies through his Spirit in you."

Romans 8:11

"Now I can see why Christ's resurrection is so important to remember," I said. "It's exactly what it will be like for us! And that brings me unspeakable joy!"

"As I said, just as God raised up Jesus, he will also raise us up by his power."

1 Corinthians 6:14

"Tell us more, Paul!"

Paul stood suddenly and cried out, "With a shouted command! With the voice of an archangel! And with the trumpet call of God…the Lord himself will descend from heaven!"

1 Thessalonians 4:16

"Jesus told people he'd be coming back that way," I said. "On the clouds of heaven!"

Matthew 24:30

"And those who died in union with Christ will rise first. For the trumpet will sound"— Paul slowly raised both hands as he spoke—"and the dead will be raised immortal."

1 Thessalonians 4:16
1 Corinthians 15:52

"And what about the living?" came a voice from the corner. I didn't catch who it was.

"Listen, and I will tell you a secret!" Paul leaned forward, his eyes wide and bright. "We will not all sleep—but we all will be changed!"

1 Corinthians 15:51

"So, if people don't die before Christ comes," I said, "like, if they're just walking around or whatever…they'll be changed?"

"In a moment, in the twinkling of an eye," Paul said. "At the last trumpet—"

"The twinkle of an eye is pretty quick," I said "Like maybe a millisecond."

1 Corinthians 15:52

"—we will be transformed."

"Why does a living body have to be changed?" someone else asked. Great question.

1 Corinthians 15:50

"This I say, friends..." Paul pointed toward the group. "Flesh and blood can have no share in the kingdom of God. Nor can the perishable share the imperishable."

I looked around again and was pleased to note that every eye in the room was locked on Paul.

1 Corinthians 15:53

"For our perishable bodies must put on an imperishable form." Paul waved a hand across the room. "These mortal bodies must put on immortality."

"And that," I said, "is why our body has to be changed. If we're still alive by then."

"Yes, and we who are still living will be caught up together in the clouds with those who died to meet the Lord in the air." Paul was smiling from ear to ear.

"So we all meet Jesus at the same time," I said. "That'll be the biggest flash mob this world has ever seen!"

1 Thessalonians 4:17

Paul's grand smile was swallowed up in a triumphant grin. "And so we shall be with the Lord forever."

"Never to die!" I said. "With a body far better than what we have now." I turned to our wandering couple, nicely settled in, back on their bench. "A body with no best-before date."

1 Corinthians 15:54

"For when this perishable has put on the imperishable, and when this mortal body has put on immortality"—Paul brought his hands down the sides of his body—"then will the words of Scripture come true." Paul threw his arms up in triumph. "Death is swallowed up in victory!"

1 Corinthians 15:55

And then a quick taunt, with Paul shaking both fists in the air. "Where, oh death, is your victory? Where, oh death, is your sting?"

"Eternal life in eternal bodies!" I said. "Why don't people get more excited about this?"

Paul sat down, looking slowly around the room. "My prayer is that the God of Jesus Christ, the Father of glory, may give you wisdom and revelation…that your hearts may be enlightened to know the hope to which you are called"—there was a sharp intake in his breath—"the riches of the glorious inheritance awaiting you." *Ephesians 1:18*

As Paul looked around once more, his eyes filled with tears. "For God has called you by our gospel to obtain the glory of our Lord Jesus Christ." *2 Thessalonians 2:14*

Paul suddenly stood again. "And thanks be to God who also gives us the victory through Christ!" He opened his arms to the whole group. "Therefore, my dear friends, stand strong and steadfast, abounding in the Lord's work, knowing that your toil is not in vain." *1 Corinthians 15:57–58*

"Why do you say our labor for the Lord not in vain?" I asked.

"Because our brief and light affliction is achieving for us a vast and transcendent glory!" *2 Corinthians 4:17*

"Sometimes our troubles can be hard to bear, Paul."

"You must be strong. Stand firm in the faith. Be watchful to not fall into sin." Paul's eyes scoured the room like a surgeon looking for tumors. "For there are many of whom I have often told you, and now tell you even with tears, who are living as enemies of the cross of Christ." *1 Corinthians 16:13* *Philippians 3:18*

"Are you talking about believers, Paul?"

"Their god is their belly. Their minds fixed on earthly things. And they glory in their shame. Their end"—Paul made a quick chopping motion—"is destruction!" *Philippians 3:19*

"Do you mean they'll be cut off from the kingdom of heaven?" I asked. "Actually, it sounds like they already are, all that focus on earthly—"

"Our citizenship, on the other hand, is in heaven, and it is from there we eagerly await our Savior, the Lord Jesus Christ." *Philippians 3:20*

"Paul, that alone strengthens me and makes me want to serve the Lord with all my heart."

Colossians 3:23–24

"Then whatever you do, do it wholeheartedly for the Lord and not for men—knowing you will receive the inheritance as your reward from the Lord." Paul pointed upwards. "For truly, you are serving the Lord Christ."

"Thank you, Paul, and good night to you. I'd like to talk more about serving the Lord—maybe next time?"

Philippians 4:23

Paul nodded in agreement. "May the grace of Jesus Christ our Lord be with all of you."

7
God's Plan for You

At one time or another, almost everyone wonders, "What does the future hold—for me?"

God says, "I know the plans I have for you, plans to prosper you and not to harm you, plans to give you hope and a future." When we read this, we often think in terms of this life: marriage, career, success, and so on.

But God is not just talking about our brief time in this broken world. Our God is an eternal, almighty God—without beginning or end. And when God thinks and makes plans, he thinks and plans in terms of eternity. So, when God says he has plans for you, they include his eternal plans for you.

The eternal design of God is so vast, so sweeping, so…cosmic, it extends to the deepest reaches of the universe, for it is his plan to make all things new! And as a child of God, you are a part of this magnificent plan. Thus, your ultimate "hope and a future" is one of immortality in a fully restored creation.

God's plan will be fulfilled at what the Bible calls "the day of the Lord," which will come suddenly and unexpectedly. At that time the heavens will pass away in roaring flames as all the elements in the universe are burned up, including the earth and everything in it. But you, and all believers, will be spared, for you are destined to share in God's divine nature and in the glory of Jesus Christ.

Throughout the New Testament, the thoughts and hearts of Christians are continually directed to the return of Jesus Christ—and the ushering in of eternal life in new heavens and a new earth. The Bible says the throne of God and of the Lamb will be there, and his servants will worship him and see his face. They will have no need of the light of a lamp, for the Lord God will be their light, and they will reign forever. This is the glorious centerpiece of the Christian hope and faith!

In the meantime, God has a plan for us in this life, here on this earth. Jesus said he came that we might have life—and have it to the full. With the gospel, God has given us everything we need to live the abundant life in Christ. We have the Holy Spirit to lead us and empower us to live a holy life, sharing the good news with others.

But how are we to know and follow God's unique plan for our life in this world? Knowing this plan can bring real meaning and value to our lives, and it was the first thing I wanted to ask the apostle Paul. There was just one problem…me.

God's Grand Plan

"Paul, I believe God wants to use me in this life—that he has a plan for me." I pulled my chair closer to the table. "But when I think of my flesh, how weak and useless it is…" I shook my head.

Romans 4:1

"What can we say, then"—Paul leaned in as though revealing a confidence—"that Abraham learned about the flesh and his own weakness?"

"Well, I know he had trouble trying to have a son."

Romans 4:17

"And yet," said Paul, "the Scriptures say God told Abraham, 'I have made you the father of many nations.'"

"But he couldn't have even one child!"

"But it is God," said Paul, "who gives life to the dead. And who calls into existence things that do not yet exist!"

Romans 8:30

"Well, that's kind of like us, I guess. The Bible says God called us and also glorified us, but I don't—"

Romans 8:29

"Indeed," said Paul, "for those God chose from the first he also destined from the first to be transformed into the image of his Son."

"Personally, I don't feel very much like Jesus. In fact, sometimes I think I'm just a filthy sinner."

"But you were washed!"

"I don't always feel so clean, Paul."

"But you were made holy!"

"I can be pretty unholy too."

"But you were pronounced righteous!" Paul grabbed my arm and shook it. "In the name of the Lord Jesus and by the Spirit of our God."

1 Corinthians 6:11

"I'm not sure I have the faith to trust in all that." I looked at Paul. "Not all the time."

"But consider Abraham!" Paul said. "God called him the father of many nations when he was about a hundred years old—and still had no child."

"Well, I'm nowhere near a hundred years old, but when I look at myself, my body, and see it's hopeless in fighting sin or doing God's will—it might as well be dead."

"And yet Abraham did not weaken in faith when he looked at his own body—which was as good as dead."

Romans 4:19

"Mind you," I said, "it was Sarah who would be having the baby."

"Nor did Abraham doubt when he thought about the deadness of Sarah's womb."

"That is exactly the kind of faith I need!" I looked around the room. "We all need!"

"Abraham had no grounds for hope," said Paul, "and yet in hope he believed—"

Romans 4:18

"That's just like us! We have no grounds for hope in ourselves"—I nodded at my Bible—"only God's promises."

"But Abraham was not divided within himself through unbelief in God's promise."

Romans 4:20

"Paul, that's it! That's the secret! He didn't allow unbelief to creep in and make him waver in double-mindedness." I shook my head again. "I do that all the time."

"It was quite the contrary," said Paul. "Praising God, Abraham was empowered by faith, being fully assured God was able to do what he promised."

Romans 4:21

"And God fulfilled his promise—they had a son, Isaac."

Galatians 3:26; 4:28

"And as for us, we also are children born in fulfillment of a promise." Paul gestured in one large sweep around the room. "For now you are sons of God through faith in Christ."

"Yet we're all so weak in our flesh," I said. "But they did have that baby, didn't they?"

I looked at the group and then at Paul. "Maybe we have to get our eyes off ourselves and onto God and his promises. Like Abraham and Sarah."

Romans 4:11

"Truly, Abraham is the father of all who have faith in God."

"Hang on there, Paul." I snatched up my Bible. "I know it talks about Sarah in here too…somewhere."

Hebrews 11:11

I fumbled through the New Testament. "Ah, here it is. The letter to the Hebrews. It says here, 'It was faith that enabled Sarah to conceive—though she was past the age for childbearing—because she considered the one who had promised to be faithful.'"

Romans 9:9

Paul nodded as though familiar with the text. He looked at me and said, "For these are the words of a promise, 'About this time I will come, and Sarah shall bear a son.'"

Hebrews 11:12

"Oh, and listen to this!" I said. "It goes on to say, 'So from one man—even when his powers were dead—there sprang a people as numerous as the stars in the heavens or the countless grains of sand upon the shore.'"

"As I told you," said Paul, "beyond all hope Abraham believed in God who brings the dead to life, and he became the father of many nations, just as God had promised."

"So can we get back to God's plan for me?" I stretched out my hand and made a fist. "What's a good promise of God I can hang onto like that—and see it fulfilled?"

2 Timothy 1:1

"The promise of eternal life in Jesus Christ."

"You didn't think very long about that, Paul."

Colossians 3:2

"I think of nothing else."

"And why is that?"

"This all will pass." Paul's fingers skimmed the tabletop, sweeping away the world and all that is in it with a casual wave of his hand. "But what is unseen…that is imperishable."

2 Corinthians 4:18

Paul had said something like that before, and I was trying to recall it when he startled me with a question.

"Do you not know that Christ's people will judge the world?"

1 Corinthians 6:2

"I know the Bible says they will reign forever."

Revelation 22:5

"And that we will also judge angels?"

1 Corinthians 6:3

"I know that Jesus said whoever overcomes the world will sit with him on his throne."

Revelation 3:21

"As God himself has said, 'Come out from the nations. Separate yourselves and touch nothing impure, and I will welcome you. I will be your Father, and you will be my sons and daughters.'"

2 Corinthians 6:17–18

"I also know God promised us an immortal body," I said. "And we'll share his glory. We just talked about that."

"Therefore, dear friends," Paul said, turning to the group, "having all these promises, let us purify ourselves from everything that pollutes our body or spirit. And in the deepest reverence for God, let us aim for perfect holiness."

2 Corinthians 7:1

"Absolutely," I said. "Who wouldn't want to sit with Jesus on his throne?"

"For this is the will of God—your holiness. Because God has not called us to a life of impurity, but to live in holiness."

1 Thessalonians 4:3, 7

"But how can we be sure of God's promises? Totally, absolutely certain—like Abraham and Sarah?"

"Because from the beginning God chose you for this salvation!" Paul's eyes blazed. "Through belief in the truth and purification by the Spirit."

2 Thessalonians 2:13

"Kind of hard to believe God would choose me," I said.

"He both saved us and called us to holiness according to his own purpose and grace." Paul turned again to the group. "Grace which was given to us in Jesus Christ before the beginning of time."

2 Timothy 1:9

"Like God chose Abraham for his own purposes?"

Genesis 18:18–19

<small>Ephesians 1:4</small>   "Just as he chose us in Christ before the creation of the world," said Paul, "that we might be holy and blameless in his sight."

I needed to get this. "Chosen by God before time. To be holy even though we can't. Like Abraham was chosen to have a son even though he couldn't—"

<small>Titus 2:14</small>   "That is why Christ gave himself for us," Paul said. "To deliver us from all wickedness and to purify his own special possession—people eager to do good."

"It looks like God went to a lot of trouble to save us and prepare us for this."

<small>Ephesians 2:10</small>   Paul laughed. "Indeed, for we are his very own workmanship, created in Jesus Christ for the good works God intended for us."

"And when you think about it," I said, "God's own sons and daughters. Quite an honor!"

Fulfilling God's Plan

A few heads bobbed in tacit accord that, upon reflection, it was in fact an honor to be called the sons and daughters of God.

<small>Ephesians 5:1–2</small>   "So then," Paul said, nodding in agreement, "as his beloved children, imitate God by walking in love."

<small>Luke 7:47</small>   "Jesus said the one who loves little has been forgiven little."

<small>Colossians 2:13</small>   Paul flashed a sidelong smile. "God has forgiven us all our sins."

"Teach us to love!" someone called out.

<small>1 Timothy 1:5</small>   "That is the purpose of all my teaching," Paul said, looking around to see who spoke. "Love that comes from a pure heart, a clear conscience, and a sincere faith."

"Paul, are you saying love comes from our faith?"

<small>1 Timothy 3:9</small>   "Holding the deep truths of the faith in a pure conscience."

"The gospel!" I said. "It's the gospel that gives us a clean conscience—no guilt!"

<small>Colossians 1:4–5</small>   Paul turned to a small knot of people seated nearest to him. "And we also have heard of your faith in Jesus Christ," he said,

smiling at them, "and the love you have for all his people because of the hope stored up for you in heaven."

I leaned over and tapped Paul on the shoulder. "Peter told believers that since they had purified their souls by the gospel, they needed to love one another fervently out of a pure heart."

1 Peter 1:22

Paul pivoted back to me, nodding. "Faith, working through love, is everything."

Galatians 5:6

"Everything?"

"For the entire law is fulfilled in one commandment." Paul held up one authoritative finger. "Love your neighbor as yourself."

Galatians 5:14

"And you can't truly love yourself without the gospel," I said. "But doing that one thing fulfills the whole law?"

"Love never wrongs a neighbor," Paul said. "Therefore, love fully satisfies the law."

Romans 13:10

"It's just hard to see how that fulfills all the law."

"I say again, the one who loves another has fulfilled the law." Paul obviously had patience, as well as love. "Therefore, owe nothing to anyone except to love one another."

Romans 13:8

"So that's all we have to do," I said. "Love each other. At least that simplifies things."

"But let your love be sincere," Paul warned. "And be full of tenderness toward one another, considering each other more highly than yourself."

Romans 12:9–10

"OK…maybe not quite so simple."

Paul smiled at me and said, "God's love has been poured out into our hearts through the Holy Spirit who was given to us." Paul turned once more to the group. "And the fruit of the Spirit is…love."

Romans 5:5
Galatians 5:22

"So it's actually God doing the loving," I said. "By his Spirit… through us."

"And now then"—Paul cleared his throat—"let everything you do be done in love."

1 Corinthians 16:14

"Can we talk about forgiveness?" I said. "It's related to love, right?"

1 Corinthians 13:5, 7 — "Truly, for love bears all things. It keeps no record of offenses."

"We just have to let God's river of love and forgiveness flow right through us to others."

Colossians 3:13 — "Yes, bearing with one another," Paul said, "and forgiving each other. If anyone has a complaint against another, just as Christ freely forgave you, so you also forgive others."

Matthew 18:22 — "If Christ forgave us everything we ever did, how can we not forgive someone else some little thing or two? Or five. Or even seventy times—"

Philippians 2:14 — "And in all that you do," said Paul, "avoid grumbling and selfish arguing."

"In other words, do everything with a cheerful and willing heart," I said.

"So that you may become blameless and pure—"

"Not tainted by selfish motives, right?"

Philippians 2:15–16 — "—spotless children of God in the midst of a crooked and corrupt generation." Paul's hands flew up, his fingers splayed. "Among whom you shine as lights in a dark world—holding fast to the message of eternal life."

"Shouldn't we hold forth the gospel as well? To other people—to bless them?"

Galatians 3:8 — "Certainly," said Paul, "for this same gospel was proclaimed beforehand to Abraham with the words, 'All the nations will be blessed through you.'"

Matthew 28:19 — "You said we're part of the eternal plan God had for Abraham." I patted my Bible. "And I know Jesus told his disciples to go and proclaim the gospel."

Galatians 3:9 — "So that all those who believe," said Paul, "are blessed with Abraham who also believed."

"So we need to hang onto the gospel message—and also hang it out there for others."

Philemon 6 — "And may the sharing of your faith lead you to recognize your full capacity for good in serving Christ."

"Just passing the blessing on," I said. "But are you saying there's more we need to do?"

Paul jerked his head toward me. "Do?"

"Yes. Do something—you know, to be holy." I regretted saying it before the words were out of my mouth.

"Can you be so foolish?" Paul shook his head in disbelief. "After beginning in the Spirit are you now perfected by the flesh?" *Galatians 3:3*

"Oh no! No, Paul. I just—"

"This one thing I want to learn from you." Paul leaned in close to me. "Did you receive the Spirit by doing the works of the law?" Paul's face loomed closer. "Or by hearing with faith?" *Galatians 3:2*

"I believed it."

"And the one who gives you the Spirit and works miracles among you"—Paul's face was now a hand's width from mine—"does he do this by works of the law or by hearing with faith?" *Galatians 3:5*

I closed my eyes. "By faith." Paul must have been satisfied with that—I heard him settle back into his chair. "But I just keep thinking I have to do something more for God."

"It is God"—did Paul snort?—"who helps you." Maybe he was just catching his breath, all that exertion. "Working in you both to will and to do for his good purpose." *Philippians 2:13*

I opened my eyes. "Did you say God gives us the desire…and the power to fulfill his plans?"

"Yes," said Paul. "In order that the righteous demands of the law might be accomplished in us."

"So the Spirit prompts. We respond. And the Spirit fulfills. Sounds perfect!"

"In us who live in obedience to the Holy Spirit," Paul added, "and not to our earthly nature." *Romans 8:4*

"Still, there must be something special we can do."

Paul frowned and looked at me sideways. His expression said that I could no more do something special than Abraham could make a baby.

"Maybe just some little thing I—we—can do? In gratitude for what God did for us."

Paul cupped his hands behind his head and leaned back in his chair, staring stoically at the ceiling.

I looked around the room. Word of these meetings had spread, and there were more people than usual. Someone had brought in an old wooden bench—seating six uncomfortably.

Paul sat up. "There is one thing."

"I knew it! Tell me." I glanced around the room. "Tell us!"

Everyone in the room leaned forward.

Paul silently studied their faces—eager, expectant. "In view of the compassion of God—"

"Yes, shown to us in his gospel," I said.

"—I urge you, by the mercies of God…"

Paul looked upward. People held their breath.

Romans 12:1

"…to offer your bodies as a living sacrifice, holy and acceptable to God." Paul raised his hands as in worship. "Your spiritual service."

All the air went out of the room.

The Holiness Path

The long bench creaked as people shifted their weight. Someone's sandal scuffed the stone floor. Off in the corner, a dog roused itself to scratch, its other leg tapping out a muted backbeat on the floor. I counted fourteen muffled drumbeats, maybe fifteen.

Romans 6:19, 21

Paul finally broke the silence. "You used to offer your bodies as servants of impurity and wickedness, leading to further wickedness." Paul caught a few averted eyes. "The end of such things is death."

Romans 6:23

Paul certainly had their attention. "For the wages of sin is death," he explained. "The gift of God, however, is everlasting life through Jesus Christ."

But he didn't have their understanding. So I leaned over toward Paul and whispered, "I don't think we're all making the connection."

"Now that you are free from the control of sin"—Paul stole a glance around the room—"you must offer your bodies to the service of righteousness, leading to holiness and eternal life." *Romans 6:22*

People were looking at each other, puzzled. "Paul, I think you left a few of us behind."

Paul backed the bus up. "Once, you were separated from God." He gestured to include everyone. "You were enemies in your mind, intent only on evil. But now God has reconciled you to himself." Paul nodded as he spoke. "He did this by the sacrifice of Christ's body in death." *Colossians 1:21*

Nice and slow—Paul was getting everybody on the bus. "God did this to present you holy, blameless, and faultless in his sight." *Colossians 1:22*

I climbed aboard too. "So now we can offer ourselves to God, holy and —"

"If—and I repeat—if," Paul said, leaning to the side like a bus driver explaining the fare, "you continue in the faith, firm and immovable, not abandoning the hope held out in the gospel." *Colossians 1:23*

I slammed the door shut. "The hope of heaven and eternal life!"

And Paul started off again. Same road, full bus. "Once you were dead in your trespasses and sins, following the ways of the world." Paul poked his thumb at himself. "We all indulged the cravings of our earthly nature." *Ephesians 2:1–3*

"Every last one of us." I poked myself.

"But God made us alive with Christ and raised us up with him." Paul pitched his hand upward. "To sit in the heavenly places in Jesus Christ." *Ephesians 2:4–6*

"When our spirit was joined with Christ's Spirit," I said. "In righteousness."

"So do not continue to offer the members of your body to sin, as instruments of unrighteousness." A few people were nodding *Romans 6:13* with Paul. "Instead, offer yourselves to God as alive from the dead, and offer your members to God as instruments of righteousness."

"Paul, you said there is a truth that produces godliness."

Titus 1:1–2 "Indeed, it is a truth based on the hope of eternal life."

"Aha," I said. "So the truth that leads to godliness is actually—"

Romans 1:16 "The gospel." Paul smiled. "For it is the power of God unto salvation."

1 Corinthians 15:1–2 Paul turned toward the room. "It is the same gospel I preached to you, which you have received and on which you stand. And by which you are being saved." Paul wagged his finger in warning. "If indeed you hold fast to the message I preached to you."

"You keep telling us to do that. Hold fast to the gospel. Stand firm in the gospel."

Romans 5:2 "Because it is only by faith in Christ that we have an entry into God's grace—in which we now stand."

Luke 18:8 "Faith," I said. "It's the one thing Jesus will be looking for when he returns to earth."

1 Timothy 6:12 "So fight the good fight of the faith," Paul said, gripping the table with both hands. "Take hold of the eternal life to which you were called."

"That's what you did, right, Paul?"

Philippians 3:12 "Not that I am already made perfect, but I press on to take hold of that for which Jesus Christ has laid hold of me."

John 15:5 "And not that we can do anything on our own anyway." I smiled knowingly at Paul. "Jesus said we can do nothing without him."

Philippians 4:13 "I can do all things through Christ," Paul said. "He strengthens me."

"But nothing without him. You said so yourself."

"Then I will gladly boast all the more of my inability." Paul laughed as though a joke was on me. "So the power of Christ may abide with me."

"Why do you say that?"

"Because the Lord said to me, 'My grace is sufficient for you, for my power is perfected in weakness.'" *2 Corinthians 12:9*

"The weaker you are?" I asked. "Or the more you realize your own weakness?"

"That is why I delight in weaknesses, ill-treatment, hardship, persecution, and suffering for the sake of Christ." Paul threw back his shoulders. "For when I am weak, it is then I am strong!" *2 Corinthians 12:10*

"Strong in the power of God," I said. "A great argument for not trying to do it ourselves."

"For that reason," said Paul, "I pray that by his power God would fulfill your every desire for goodness and your every action inspired by faith." *2 Thessalonians 1:11*

I rested my hand on my Bible. "The psalmist says if we commit our way to the Lord and trust in him, the Lord will make our righteousness shine like the noonday sun." *Psalm 37:5–6*

"Truly, the God of peace himself will make you perfect in holiness," Paul said, "and your entire spirit, soul, and body kept blameless at the coming of Jesus Christ, our Lord." *1 Thessalonians 5:23*

"We can trust God to do all that?"

"He who calls you is absolutely to be trusted," Paul said, "and he will do it." *1 Thessalonians 5:24*

"Then why is it so hard for us to commit our way to God?" I asked no one in particular. "It's nothing more than handing our life and future into his care. Who better to work that out?"

Paul gave me an approving smile and turned to the group. "So now, dear friends, work out your salvation to the finish, anxious to do right—for it is God who is at work within you, both to will and to work." *Philippians 2:12–13*

"Let's entrust ourselves to God," I said, "expecting to see his awesome power in action!"

"And I pray you may be filled with the knowledge of his will in true spiritual wisdom," Paul said, "strengthened with his power for all endurance and perseverance." *Colossians 1:11*

"Sounds like this is how we can find and follow God's plans for us." I looked around the room. "And who knows what desires he might place in our heart? To bless others."

Colossians 1:12

"Joyfully giving thanks to the Father," said Paul, "who has made you fit to share in the inheritance of Christ's people in the realms of light."

"Trusting and praising God like Abraham and Sarah did!"

Colossians 1:10
1 Thessalonians 2:12

"So that you may walk worthy of the Lord," Paul said, "fully pleasing to God who calls you into his own kingdom and glory—bearing fruit in every good work."

"Paul, that is your secret of a victorious Christian life!" My mind bounced back to our first meeting. "You've answered our question of how to live a life that pleases God! Thank you from all of us. Thank you—and good night, dear friend."

2 Thessalonians 1:2

Paul turned in his seat, beaming like someone who had just fulfilled a splendid promise. "Grace and peace to you all from God our Father and Jesus Christ our Lord."

Epilogue
Famous Last Words

It was quite a journey—exploring Paul's gospel with him. Hearing about his Jewish life and startling conversion to Christianity. Talking about the deadly defect in people and how God issued a worldwide recall offering to fix it—free. And the need for us to respond to God's call to repent and trust in Jesus Christ for salvation.

I wasn't surprised by the uncertainty among the Jews as to whether Jesus was their long-awaited Messiah—people still wonder about that today! But Paul proved that Jesus of Nazareth is in fact the Christ, and he described in detail both our Savior's mission and the miracle of his resurrection.

Paul went on to describe the believer as a new creation in Christ, with supernatural power and freedom from the control of sin. And he listed the amazing differences between the physical realm of creation and the spiritual realm of God. Paul's stunning revelations of the glorious realities of what God has done in and for those who believe in Jesus made me want to dance!

And then the conversation I'd been waiting for: how to use and apply the fundamental truths about the kingdom of God and who we are in Christ. Paul carefully explained how to knit these truths into our Christian life and how to walk in Holy Spirit power to achieve victory in our day-to-day lives.

Paul got pretty excited when he talked about the triumph over death that all believers will share. And as he confirmed our hope of eternal life, I'll never forget his passionate description of how our bodies will be transformed into the likeness of Christ's own glorious body—when Jesus comes back to save all those who received his gospel.

As Paul talked about God's ultimate plan for humankind—and for all of creation—I had a staggering insight. I realized we must know God's plan for us in eternity before we can know and fulfill his plans for us in this life! We first have to know God personally and experience his cleansing power and Holy Spirit within us. And with that settled, I was determined to follow Paul's practical advice on knowing and fulfilling God's unique plans for me.

Now, in my final visit with Paul, I dropped in to say goodbye—although I did have a couple of follow-up questions for him. And, as it turned out, one other question that surprised even me.

A Precious Jewel

I sat on the edge of my chair, as though I'd be leaving any minute. "Paul, do you remember we talked earlier about the gospel having many different facets, like a sparkling diamond?"

Ephesians 1:13 — "Truly, for it is the good news of your salvation."

"Yes, salvation itself is a facet!" I said. "God sent Christ to save us, plus all of creation."

Romans 10:8 — "That is the message of faith that we preach."

"And right there is another facet of the gospel—faith!"

Romans 10:10 — "Faith, indeed," said Paul. "For it is with the heart that one believes and is declared righteous."

Ephesians 2:8 — "Righteousness and salvation by faith—that's the gospel."

2 Timothy 2:9
2 Corinthians 4:1 — "For which I suffer hardships," Paul said, "even to being chained as a criminal. But having this ministry, and as I have received mercy, I do not lose heart." Paul looked up sharply. "Besides, the word of God is not in chains."

"The gospel cannot be restrained," I said, "for it's the word and power of God himself! Peter and Luke said it was the word of the Lord, and I think you called it the word of Christ."

Colossians 3:16 — "And you must let this word of Christ abide in you richly," said Paul, "teaching and exhorting one another with psalms and hymns and sacred songs. Singing to God by the grace in your hearts."

"God's grace deep in our heart!" I leaned over and whispered to Paul, "I love how you turn everything into a sermon." I swung around to the group to underline the bottom line. "We have to get these gospel truths from our heads down into our hearts. All of us!"

"Yes, so that you may do good," Paul said, "rich in good deeds, generous and eager to share, treasuring up for yourselves a good foundation for the future, to take hold of eternal life." *1 Timothy 6:18–19*

"Eternal life! See? All these lovely facets of the gospel."

"I also called the gospel the word of truth." *Colossians 1:5*

"And truth it is! Paul, I think you're enjoying this."

"How he has loved us!" Paul sighed and sat back in his chair. "Giving us eternal comfort and good hope by grace." *2 Thessalonians 2:16*

Paul and I sat there, looking around the room, nodding and basking in the love of God.

"So the gospel," I said, "can be described as God's message of salvation, of his mercy and grace, as the word of truth…of cleansing from sin and the gift of righteousness"—I took a quick breath—"and of our inheritance, the hope of eternal life. All through faith in Jesus Christ."

"And having believed in him," said Paul, "you were sealed with the Holy Spirit." *Ephesians 1:13*

I looked at Paul. "You're good at piling words together. Think you can bundle all that into one short message?"

Paul didn't even blink. "Because of his mercy God saved us by the washing and renewing of the Holy Spirit poured out through Jesus Christ our Savior"—Paul spread his arms out toward the group—"and having pronounced us righteous by his grace, he made us heirs of the hope of eternal life." *Titus 3:4–7*

"Impressive!" I said. "A sermon in a sentence."

Paul smiled. "It is a trustworthy saying." *Titus 3:8*

"But I think we missed faith and truth."

Paul was ready for me. "That all those who did not have faith in the truth, but took pleasure in wickedness, may be condemned." *2 Thessalonians 2:12*

Famous Last Words

"Because they kept sinning?"

"Because they did not believe the gospel." Paul turned toward me, his face radiant. "For Scripture says, 'All who believe in him shall not be put to shame.'"

Romans 10:11

"That's the good news, for sure." I nodded. "And Jesus himself said that those who do not believe will be condemned. So I know you're right to warn people, but—"

"If we endure, we will reign together with him." Paul turned his hands palms up and shrugged his shoulders. "But if we deny him, he will deny us."

2 Timothy 2:12

"Endure?"

"There will be immortality for those who persevere in doing good, pursuing glory, honor, and eternal life." Paul's eyes swept the room. "Therefore, let us not tire of doing right, for at the proper season we will reap our harvest. He shook his finger. "If we do not grow weary!"

Romans 2:7
Galatians 6:9

"And if we deny him?"

"Wrath and rage await those who are self-seeking, refusing to obey the truth, and instead yield to unrighteousness." Paul was still wagging his warning finger. "Do not be deceived! God cannot be mocked. What a man sows, he will reap."

Romans 2:8
Galatians 6:7

"Paul, I think you're starting to scare—"

"For whoever sows to the flesh will from that same flesh reap corruption." Paul was frantically shaking and pointing his finger around the room. "But the one who sows to the Spirit will from that same Spirit reap eternal life."

Galatians 6:8

Making people uncomfortable was obviously not an issue for Paul. I should have known that by this time. "OK!" I said. "Fair enough. I guess everyone needs to understand what's at stake here. Either to be gained or…lost."

"As a messenger of the gospel," Paul continued, "you must be ready whether in season or out to admonish, rebuke, and exhort with all forbearance and instruction."

2 Timothy 4:2

God's Amazing Grace

I had hoped to end our time together on a high note. How to pull this one back? I ran the fingers of both hands through my hair and clasped them behind my head…

"Paul, I just had a thought! There are many different words to describe the gospel. All of them good and true! But if you had to reduce the entire gospel message to one word—just one word—what would it be?"

Paul angled his head and eyes sharply downward and thought for a moment. He was taking my question seriously, as he took all of my questions. Then he looked up toward heaven. "Grace!" he cried exultantly. "For the grace of God has now appeared with salvation for all." *Titus 2:11*

"Of course!" I said. "For the gospel is the full manifestation of God's grace toward us."

"Praise the glory of God's grace!" said Paul. "For it is by grace he has made us accepted in the beloved!" *Ephesians 1:6*

"Accepted in Jesus," I said. "That's the whole gospel in a nutshell, isn't it?"

"Truly," Paul said, "for in him and the shedding of his blood we are restored to God by the forgiveness of our sins. All according to the abundant riches…of God's grace." *Ephesians 1:7*

"Amazing grace!" I said. "It sets us free from the guilt of sin and gives us eternal life."

Paul sat up straight, his eyes flashing. "That in the ages to come God might display the boundless riches of his grace toward us in Jesus Christ." *Ephesians 2:7*

"Yes, God's grace offered in the gospel—a gift wrapped in mercy and love." I leaned in toward Paul. "You said it was grace that enabled you to cope with all that you…endured." *1 Corinthians 15:10*

"Indeed, for our glorying is in this," Paul said, "that in the world we acted in purity and godly sincerity, not based on fleshly wisdom, but by the grace of God." *2 Corinthians 1:12*

"And what did that look like?"

1 Corinthians 4:12–13

"Meeting abuse with blessings. And meeting persecution with endurance. Meeting slander with gentle appeals."

"But that has to wear you down, no?"

2 Corinthians 4:8–9

"No. Though hard pressed on every side, we are not crushed. Though at wit's end, we are not driven to despair." Paul stiffened. "Though struck down, we are not destroyed."

"Still, it sounds pretty depressing to me."

2 Corinthians 6:10

"Thrown into sorrow, yet we are always rejoicing. Destitute in poverty, we enrich many. As having nothing, yet possessing everything!"

"How on earth—"

1 Corinthians 15:10

"As I said, it was not me—but the grace of God which was with me."

"And that must be why you keep saying, 'The grace of the Lord be with you.'"

2 Corinthians 9:8

"For we know God can make his grace overflow unto you too, that you may have an abundance of grace for every good work."

"It sounds like there's a lot of power in God's grace," I said. "Enough for us in this world!"

2 Corinthians 12:9

"As Jesus himself said to me, 'My grace is sufficient for you, for my power is—'"

"Perfected in our weakness, yes," I said. "But I see it is unleashed by our faith in the gospel."

Paul turned to the group, both eyebrows raised.

"When I think of the Lord's grace," I explained, "I think of the gospel which is the demonstration of his grace. So, when Jesus says his grace is sufficient, it's like saying his death, his forgiveness, his salvation—really, his gospel is sufficient for us!"

2 Timothy 2:1

"So you then," said Paul, "be strong in the power of the grace that is in Jesus Christ."

Hebrews 10:29

"And it's real power," I said. "The writer of the letter to the Hebrews even referred to the Spirit of grace. That's divine power right there!"

"Because the kingdom of God," said Paul, "does not operate in words—but in power." *1 Corinthians 4:20*

"Right! And you have said the gospel itself is the power of God working for our salvation." *Romans 1:16*

"And this gospel is bearing fruit and increasing throughout the world just as it is among you"—Paul looked around the room—"from the day you heard it and understood the grace of God as it truly is." *Colossians 1:5–6*

"Once you get a hold of the gospel," I said, turning to the group, "it gets a hold of you!" I turned back to Paul. "And that must be why you told the new believers in Antioch to abide in the grace of God they received in the gospel." *Acts 13:43*

"But then," Paul said, surveying the room, "I know there are those who want to distort the gospel of Christ. I have said it before, and I say it again—if anyone preaches a gospel other than what you received, may he be accursed!" *Galatians 1:7, 9*

"And that's why the Bible warns us not to be led away by other teachings," I said, "and reminds us it's good for the heart to be strengthened by grace." *Hebrews 13:9*

"And much more," said Paul, "for those who receive God's overflowing grace and his gift of righteousness will reign in life through Jesus Christ." *Romans 5:17*

"Reign in life indeed!" I said, standing for an announcement. "Since God's grace has now been revealed in the gospel"—I glanced back at Paul—"we need to stand in it every hour."

"For his grace trains us to deny ungodliness and worldly desire." Paul was right with me. "And with self-control to live upright and godly lives." *Titus 2:12*

"But only as we live and walk every minute in his grace," I said. "In his gospel!"

"And now," said Paul, standing up as well, "I commend you—all of you—to God and to the message of his grace, which has the power to build you up and give you an eternal inheritance with all those who are made holy." *Acts 20:32*

Paul's Final Advice

Midmorning sunlight was flooding the room, and I wasn't sure whether the warmth I felt was from the sun or from an overwhelming sense of God's love. Maybe it was both.

But I knew I'd be leaving soon. "Paul, you have been so helpful to me and to so many of us here. Just before I go, do you have one or two pieces of advice?"

1 Thessalonians 5:16–17, 19, 21

Paul started counting off with his fingers, starting with his little finger and working up. "Rejoice at all times. Pray constantly. Do not quench the Spirit. Hold fast to what is good—"

"That's, like, five or—"

1 Thessalonians 5:22

"Forsake every kind of evil."

I admired Paul's broad focus on the subject of godliness. "Those are all very important, to be sure," I said. "But I was just looking for a couple of things to really hold on to."

Romans 12:12

Paul sat down slowly, and very deliberately. He seemed to be concentrating on my question, but I noted he was careful not to put weight on his right hip. "What to hold on to," he repeated, nodding gently as he spoke. "Why…rejoicing in hope!"

1 Peter 1:8

"Ah, yes," I said. "Rejoicing in the hope of eternal life. With an inexpressible joy, as the apostle Peter put it."

1 Peter 1:6

Why was Paul favoring his right side? And why didn't I notice it earlier? I sat down and leaned in close toward Paul. "Even though, as Peter also said, you may have suffered various trials."

Paul closed his eyes and gently folded his hands. "All the while, persevering steadfastly in prayer."

"I know we should be doing more of that," I said. "We say it's the most important thing."

Colossians 4:2

"Devote yourselves to prayer," Paul said, opening his eyes, now glistening with tears. "Be diligent in prayer, with thanksgiving."

"Though we often seem to leave it to the last."

Ephesians 6:18

"Pray in the Spirit at all times," Paul added. "Be intent upon this, making heartfelt appeals for all Christ's people."

"A lot more prayer," I said. "There's something to hold on to."

I was preparing to leave. "And you, Paul? What's next for you?"

"As for me"—Paul pursed his lips and tilted his head—"I have fought the good fight. I finished the race. I kept the faith.

Paul looked up to heaven. "And now the crown of righteousness awaits me, which the Lord, the just judge, will give me on that day." Paul lowered his gaze and slowly scanned the room. "And not only to me, but to all who long for his appearing."

"That's so you, Paul. Always thinking of other people and their eternal future."

"I do not count my life of value to myself…only to complete the course set before me." Paul looked me squarely in the eye. "And the task I received from the Lord Jesus to declare the good news of the grace of God."

"Oh, Paul…Paul. You *were* faithful. And you have scattered the gospel of God's grace further than you know."

I stood and took a last look around. The people were as still as statues, fixed in awe and admiration. "Paul, you've been a rich blessing to me—to us. We thank you."

The statues began to stir, and an epidemic of approving nods and appreciative smiles broke out all around the room.

I placed my hand on Paul's shoulder, gave a light squeeze, and headed for the door. "Goodbye, Paul."

A few people got up to say goodbye to me, including the wandering couple, who walked me toward the door.

"Rejoice in the Lord always," Paul shouted after me. "I say it again, rejoice!"

As I opened the door to leave, Paul cried out, "…in his grace!"

Those three little words ricocheted like pebbles off the stone walls of the house. They continued to rattle around in my head as I closed the door and started down the path.

Before I got to the end of the path, they had tumbled into my soul.

And all the way home, they sang in my heart like a choir.

2 Timothy 4:7

2 Timothy 4:8

Acts 20:24

Philippians 4:4

Ask the Apostle

Study Guide

Your Bible is a source of spiritual strength. Because it is the living word of God, it is both a resource and a lifeline for your Christian walk.

The statements made by Paul in this book are taken directly from the Bible. As you enter into these conversations, you enter into a direct encounter with Scripture to help you understand the full gospel message and apply it to your life. This study guide directs you back to the source of Paul's statements, right in your own Bible.

Using the study guide to strengthen your faith can be an enjoyable and spiritually invigorating experience—for either individual or group study. Each chapter in the book includes an introduction and three segments of dialogue. Read one section at a time and then turn to the questions for that section in the study guide to help you process and clarify the key teachings presented by Paul.

To use the book and study guide most effectively in a group setting, I recommend that people take turns reading from the dialogue: one in the role of Paul and one in the role of the narrator. In a larger group setting, you may have people 'act out' Paul and the narrator, sitting at a small table with a Bible and a cup on it.

This study guide introduces a unique 'Ask the Apostle' feature. At the end of each section is a relevant question for the group to discuss and then refer to the Bible for an answer from one of Paul's letters. Someone from the group can read the answer to the question (as Paul), and then the group can consider his answer and discuss the follow-up question based on Paul's response.

At the end of each section, you can also open up the discussion to anything people might want to talk about regarding something that either Paul or the narrator said during their conversation.

Have fun as you learn and build your faith in the greatest message in the world—the gospel!

Chapter One
Paul and His Gospel

Chapter Introduction

Key Bible Verses

Acts 13:1–5, 49, 52; 14:21–23; 15:36; 16:4–5, 14–15; 17:1–4; 18:1–8, 24–28; 19:1–8; 20:17–21, 29–31; 28:30–31

- What did evangelism and discipleship look like for the first Christians?
- What was the force behind this work? What was the fruit?
- What do you think Christian evangelism and discipleship could look like today?
- What part of the cry for more faith, more power, and more of Jesus resonates most with you?

Paul and the Law

1. **Read Romans 3:1–2; 9:4**
   - When we become a Christian, should we be ashamed of our prior religious tradition?
   - Do we need to be embarrassed if we do not have a prior religious tradition?

2. **Read Acts 8:1, 3**
   - Why did Paul and the Jewish leaders persecute Christians?
   - Is it surprising that Christians are still being persecuted today? Galatians 4:29; 1 John 3:12–13

3. **Read Acts 22:3–4; 26:10–11**
   - How is it that people can be zealous for God and yet imprison and kill others who love God? Acts 7:57–60; 9:1–2, 21

4. **Read Romans 3:20**
   - What were the purposes of the law God gave to Moses? Galatians 3:19, 23–24

5. **Read Galatians 2:21; 3:21**
   - What did Paul mean by these statements?

ASK THE APOSTLE

- Can righteousness and heaven be attained through obedience to the law?
- Discuss as a group, and then read aloud Paul's answer from Romans 3:19–20.
- Are there areas in your life where you still think you need to be or do better to enter heaven?

Paul Meets Jesus

1. **Read Acts 22:4–10**
   - What is most striking to you about Paul's encounter with Jesus?
   - Why did that meeting cause such a dramatic change in Paul?
   - Did Paul meet Jesus before or after the Lord's death?
   - Is it possible for people to meet Jesus today?
   - How might such a meeting be different from Paul's?
   - How might it be the same?

2. **Read 1 Timothy 1:12–16**
   - Why did Paul say he was the worst of sinners?
   - Why was Paul shown mercy?
   - What do these verses mean for people today?
   - Why did Ananias tell Paul to be baptized? Acts 22:16
   - What are the implications of this verse for believers today?

3. **Read Galatians 2:1–5**
   - Paul had a strong disagreement with some Jewish Christians about circumcision. Why did Paul dispute this tradition?
   - What part of a person must be circumcised in order to be a true disciple of Jesus? Romans 2:29
   - Were there other false teachings among believers in Paul's time?
   - Are there false teachings within the body of Christ today?
   - If so, what could you do about that?

4. **Read Galatians 1:11–12; 2:6–9**
   - Who did Paul receive his gospel message from? Acts 22:14-15; 26:15–16
   - If Paul received the gospel message from Jesus himself, and the gospel Paul taught was personally confirmed by the apostles James, Peter, and John, do you think it is trustworthy?
   - Jesus told Paul he was sending him to others to open their eyes and turn them from darkness to light. Before that could take place, what had to happen to Paul and his own eyes? Acts 26:17–18
   - Is that still a necessary step for people to be saved today?

NOTES

ASK THE APOSTLE

- What is the gospel in a nutshell?
- Discuss as a group, and then read aloud Paul's answer from Titus 3:4–7.
- Would you add anything to Paul's description?

Paul's Gospel Ministry

1. **Read 2 Corinthians 11:23–28**
   - What were some of the difficult circumstances Paul encountered in sharing the gospel message?
   - What are some of the difficulties you encounter in telling others the good news of Christ?
   - Paul suffered a great deal for the sake of the gospel and for the Jesus he loved. Do you think there is a connection between Paul enduring much and Christ forgiving him much?

2. **Read 1 Corinthians 15:10**
   - What did Paul mean when he said, "It was the grace of God with me"?
   - What are some ways this grace of God gave Paul strength and endurance?
   - Could this work the same way for Christians today?

3. **Read Acts 17:2–4**
   - Why did Paul use the Scriptures to convince the Jews that Jesus was the Messiah?
   - Can we use the Bible in the same way to persuade people that Jesus is the Messiah?
   - What are some other ways we might be able to do that?

4. **Read 2 Corinthians 5:14–15**
   - Facing death or prison at every turn, Paul said he was compelled to share the gospel. What was compelling him?
   - What compels you to share the gospel message with family and friends?

ASK THE APOSTLE

- Why did Paul say those who are saved should no longer live for themselves?

- Discuss as a group, and then read aloud Paul's answer from Romans 14:7–9.

- Is this true of everyone who is born again?

Chapter Two
The World's Greatest Recall

Chapter Introduction

Key Bible Verses

Ezekiel 18:30–32; Matthew 4:12–17; Mark 6:12; Acts 2:38; 3:19; 2 Peter 3:9

- Do you believe all people are born with the defect the Bible calls sin?
- What are the differences and similarities between this flaw in people and a defect in a vehicle?
- What approaches have you—or others—tried over the years to 'repair' themselves?
- How successful have we been with that repair job?
- Can this human defect be fixed without God?

The Fatal Defect

1. **Read Romans 3:10–18**
   - Is this Biblical account an accurate portrayal of the human condition?
   - Is there anything you can add to this list?
   - Can people go through their entire life without knowing they have this deadly defect?
   - Why do you suppose many people believe we are all basically born good?

2. **Read Romans 1:28–32**
   - How do you feel when you read these verses?
   - Why do people get upset when they hear or read these words?
   - Why do people not like to talk about the fact that they are born sinners?

- Was—or is—it hard for you to talk about that?

3. **Read Romans 3:23; 14:23**
   - What is sin?
   - Why does Paul say that whatever is not of faith is sin?
   - Does God see us differently depending on how much we have sinned?
   - Will this world ever be free of sin?

4. **Read Ephesians 4:17–19**
   - How does our sin separate us from God?
   - What is the consequence of that separation?

ASK THE APOSTLE

- Why did it not bother Paul to talk about sin, and how might he advise us in that area?
- Discuss as a group, and then read aloud Paul's answer from 2 Corinthians 2:17 and 2 Timothy 2:15.
- What is the source of Paul's boldness in confronting sin?

In Bondage to Sin

1. **Read Romans 7:15**
   - It is often said that one of the steps to salvation in Jesus Christ is to know you're a sinner and there is nothing you can do about it. Do you agree with this statement? Romans 5:6
   - Can a good upbringing, knowing right from wrong, or determination free us from the chains of sin? Why or why not?
   - Do you think some people have too many sins for God to forgive them? Romans 5:20–21

NOTES

2. **Read Romans 7:18–19**
   - Is this a good test to help people recognize whether they have the sin defect?
   - In what ways are we in bondage to sin?

3. **Read Romans 5:12, 19**
   - How did we get into this 'sin' situation? Genesis 3:1–19

4. **Read Romans 7:24; 8:1**
   - Discuss the elements of repentance and faith in these two statements of Paul.

5. **Read 1 Corinthians 15:9**
   - Why would Paul say he is the least of the apostles? Galatians 1:13; Acts 26:9–10
   - When God chose Paul to be his messenger of the gospel, he chose a murderer. He chose a man who was religious but far from the religion Jesus Christ had brought. What does that show us about God's grace and who he is willing to accept as his own through faith in his Son?

6. **Read Romans 8:2**
   - Paul proclaimed that the power of the life-giving Spirit in Jesus Christ set him free from the power of sin and death. Can believers expect to experience that same freedom today?
   - How have you experienced freedom from the power of sin?

ASK THE APOSTLE

- What could we say to someone struggling with turning from sin?
- Discuss as a group, and then read aloud Paul's answer from 2 Corinthians 5:20–21; 6:1–2.
- Can you see yourself saying something like that to somebody?

True Repentance

1. **Read 2 Corinthians 7:9–11**
   - What is the difference between worldly sorrow and godly sorrow?
   - What is the evidence of a godly sorrow?

2. **Read Ezekiel 33:10–11**
   - What does God require of people with respect to their evil ways?
   - Why does God command this?

3. **Read Acts 26:17–20; Luke 19:8–10**
   - What does Jesus mean by "turn from darkness to light"?
   - What are two key elements of true repentance? Acts 26:19–20
   - How did Zacchaeus demonstrate that he had repented of his sins?
   - How did Jesus respond to this change of heart?

4. **Read Acts 17:30–31; Romans 2:8–9; 6:16, 23; 14:10–12**
   - Why must we repent?
   - How would you explain repentance to a young child?
   - Is it true that deep down we know many of our actions are wrong?
   - Why did Paul become frustrated when people refused to acknowledge their sin and turn from it?
   - Why is it so hard for people to repent?
   - Was—or is—it hard for you to repent?

5. **Read Mark 1:14–15**
   - What two things are required for salvation?
   - John the Baptist called people to repentance, and then he pointed them to Jesus. Should we still be using that evangelism model today?

NOTES

ASK THE APOSTLE

- How do you think God feels about people hearing his gospel?
- Discuss as a group, and then read aloud Paul's answer from Romans 10:11–13 and 1 Timothy 2:3–4.
- How does this affect your desire and confidence to share the gospel with others?

Chapter Three
The Messiah Comes

Chapter Introduction

Key Bible Verses

Isaiah 9:6–7; 35:5–6; 42:1–4; 53:1, 11; Psalm 2:7; 16:10; 72:12–13; 110:1; John 1:10–11, 19–20, 31–33; Luke 3:15–16; 7:19, 22; Matthew 16:13–15

- Why was there so much uncertainty as to who the Messiah was—or whether he had even come?
- Who do people today say Jesus is?
- Do you think there will always be people who doubt that Jesus is the Messiah? Why?

Who is the Messiah?

1. **Read John 1:41; 4:25**
   - What do the words "Messiah" and "Christ" mean?
   - What were some expectations of the coming Messiah?

2. **Read Romans 1:3–4; 1 Timothy 3:16**
   - How can we know for certain that Jesus is fully God and fully man?

3. **Read Colossians 1:15–16; 2:9**
   - What ultimately proves the divinity of Jesus, the man?
   - Why was it necessary that Jesus be fully human and fully God?

4. **Read Luke 3:15–16**
   - Why would people think John the Baptist was the Messiah?
   - What was John the Baptist's true role?
   - What kind of baptism could the Messiah give that John the Baptist could not?

5. **Read Philippians 2:6–8; Colossians 1:19–20; Acts 17:2–3**
   - Why did Jesus come to earth?
   - Jesus was a Jew. Did he die for the Jews only? 1 John 2:2
   - What is God's plan for the Gentiles, the non-Jews? Ephesians 3:6
   - What was God's ultimate plan for his Messiah? Ephesians 1:10

6. **Read Isaiah 53:5, 10–11; Acts 13:27**
   - What do some of the Jewish prophecies say about the Messiah?
   - How does Paul explain the fact that people did not recognize Jesus as the Messiah?
   - Why are the prophecies concerning Jesus still not understood or accepted today, even though many of them have been fulfilled?

ASK THE APOSTLE

- Jesus Christ saved people, but what will become of the fallen world we live in?
- Discuss as a group, and then read aloud Paul's answer from Romans 8:20–21.
- Hearing Paul's answer, how does it make you feel to be a Christian?

God's Secret Plan

1. **Read 2 Timothy 1:9–10; 1 Corinthians 6:14**
   - What was God's eternal plan for his chosen ones?
   - What did Paul mean when he said, "Christ destroyed death"?
   - If Christ destroyed death, why are people still dying? 1 Corinthians 6:14; 15:23, 26

2. **Read Mark 15:25–27**
   - Many people were crucified in the time of Jesus. What was different about his crucifixion and death?
   - What is the proof that our sins have been forgiven? Romans 4:24–25

3. **Read 1 Corinthians 15:21**
   - Who are the two men Paul is talking about in this verse?
   - How does this statement summarize the fall and restoration of humankind? Romans 5:21

4. **Read Matthew 5:20**
   - How much righteousness does a person need to enter heaven and the presence of God?
   - How can we achieve a level of perfect righteousness? Romans 3:21–22
   - Why did the Pharisees and other Jews miss out on God's plan of salvation? Romans 10:2–4
   - Do you know people who are missing out on salvation for that same reason?
   - What could you tell them?

5. **Read Romans 9:31–33; Acts 16:31**
   - What or who is the stumbling stone Paul referred to?
   - How and why do people stumble at this stone today?
   - How could you help people believe in Jesus for salvation?

NOTES

ASK THE APOSTLE

♦ How does the resurrection of Jesus prove we are forgiven by God?

♦ Discuss as a group, and then read aloud Paul's answer from Acts 13:36–39.

♦ Does this explanation satisfy your conscience?

That Elusive Faith

1. **Read Hebrews 11:1**
   - How would you define Biblical faith?
   - What is the source and nature of this faith? Galatians 5:22; Romans 12:3; Hebrews 12:2

2. **Read Ephesians 2:8; Matthew 16:16–17**
   - How does faith in Jesus as the divine Messiah come into a person's life? 1 Corinthians 12:3
   - How did it come into your life?

3. **Read 2 Corinthians 4:3–4; Matthew 13:14–19**
   - Why do some people not recognize Jesus as the Messiah, the son of God?
   - What do these people say about Jesus?
   - Why does faith not come into everyone's life through the gospel?
   - Is there anything you can do about that?

4. **Read 1 John 4:9; 2 Corinthians 5:19, 21**
   - How did God show his love for the world? Romans 5:8
   - What was the price God paid for the church? Acts 20:28; Colossians 2:9

5. **Read Romans 8:38–39**
   - What can separate believers from the love of God shown in his Messiah?
   - Do you believe this? If so, is there somebody you need to tell about God's love?

ASK THE APOSTLE

- What is it that Satan does not want people to know?
- Discuss as a group, and then read aloud Paul's answer from 2 Corinthians 5:18–19.
- How can you counter Satan's attempts to hold back this good news?

NOTES

Chapter Four
A New and Improved You

Chapter Introduction

Key Bible Verses

John 3:1–6; Matthew 12:28; 21:28–32; Mark 4:11; 10:15; Luke 7:28; 8:1; 12:29–32; 16:16; 17:20–21

- How long has the human quest for a new and improved self been going on?
- What are some of the popular self-help concepts and programs—and their results?
- What are the differences and similarities between the physical self and the new spiritual self?

A New Creation

1. **Read Galatians 3:26–27**
   - How do we become children of God?

2. **Read 1 Corinthians 12:12–14**
   - What did Paul mean when he said believers were all given to drink of one Spirit?
   - If we are each a child of God, how is it that we are one body in Christ?
   - If you are in God's family, you will have brothers and sisters. What are the implications of this fact to you as a Christian?

3. **Read 2 Corinthians 5:17**
   - How does the new creation happen? Ephesians 1:13
   - We do not have any control over our physical birth. Is this true of our spiritual birth as well?

4. **Read Ephesians 4:24; Galatians 5:22–23**
   - When we are born physically, we inherit some of the characteristics of our parents. What traits do we receive from our heavenly Father when we are born spiritually?
   - How do these new qualities come to us?

5. **Read Romans 2:25–29**
   - What is the difference between the circumcision of the law and the circumcision of the Spirit? Deuteronomy 30:6
   - How would you explain circumcision of the heart to a young child? Colossians 2:11–13

6. **Read Romans 6:6–7**
   - What became of our 'old' self when Jesus was crucified?
   - Why is sin no longer master over a believer?
     Romans 6:1–3, 17–18; 8:2–3

7. **Read Romans 6:8–10**
   - When we are born physically, we know it: consider the wonder in a baby's eyes seeing the world for the first time. Can we experience a spiritual birth and not know it?
   - What are some things we 'see' for the first time after our spiritual birth?
   - William Tyndale, an English scholar who translated the Bible into English in the early 1500s, said the gospel signifies "good, merry, glad, and joyful tidings that maketh a man's heart glad and maketh him sing, dance, and leap for joy."
     (*William Tyndale: A Biography*, Yale University Press)
   - Tyndale was burned at the stake in 1536, a martyr for the faith. What do you suppose he would say to someone who was unsure about his or her faith?

ASK THE APOSTLE

- How can we know for certain we are children of God?
- Discuss as a group, and then read aloud Paul's answer from Romans 8:14–17.
- Do you have and enjoy the inner witness of this truth?

SPIRITUAL SECRETS

1. **Read 1 Corinthians 2:9–16**
   - Why is it difficult for people to receive and understand spiritual truths?
   - What are some differences between the natural person and the spiritual person?

2. **Read 1 Corinthians 3:16**
   - What is the source of the supernatural power available to Christian believers? 2 Corinthians 4:7
   - How great or potent is this power? Ephesians 1:19–20; 3:20
   - How is this power revealed in Christians? 2 Timothy 1:7
   - When we were born into the world, we were freed from the constraints of our mother's womb and entered into an expansive universe. What were we freed from in the womb when we passed into the physical world?
   - When we were born again into the kingdom of God, we entered into the eternal vastness of a spiritual realm. What were we freed from in the physical world when we gained access to this spiritual realm?

3. **Read Galatians 4:6; Colossians 1:26–27**
   - What are some effects of the Spirit of Jesus Christ being in a person?
   - What is the believer's "hope of glory"? Romans 5:2; Ephesians 1:18

4. **Read Colossians 2:9–10 and 1 Corinthians 2:3–5**
   - If all the fullness of God is in Christ, and if Christ is in you, are you lacking anything?
   - The apostle Paul demonstrated divine power when he proclaimed the gospel. How can we release this same power in our lives? 2 Corinthians 12:9–10
   - Does the manifestation of Christ's power in our lives depend on how weak we are, or on how much we realize our own weakness?

5. **Read Matthew 4:1–11**
   - When Satan tempted Jesus in the wilderness, the Lord used the word of God as his protection. Jesus made it clear to Satan that his trust and commitment were to God and his word. If we respond to Satan's temptations like Jesus did, will Satan leave us as well?
   - Can we expect angels to come and minister to us?
     Hebrews 1:13–14

6. **Read Philippians 2:8–11; Ephesians 1:22–23**
   - God gave us his Son, scorned and debased in death for our salvation. And now he has once more given us his Son, exalted in life to the highest places and honors for our glory.
   - What do we do with *that*?
   - What are *you* doing with that?

NOTES

ASK THE APOSTLE

- Why is the Bible vital to a Christian's life and walk?
- Discuss as a group, and then read aloud Paul's answer from 2 Timothy 3:16–17.
- What are some of the ways the Bible helps you in your Christian walk?

SPIRITUAL BLESSINGS

1. **Read Galatians 2:20**
   - If Paul's approach to living in this world worked for him, can it also work for us?
   - Why did Paul continually pray and labor for believers that Christ would dwell in their hearts through faith?
     Ephesians 3:14–17; Galatians 4:19

- If the things of the Spirit are invisible, how can others see Christ in you?

2. **Read Galatians 5:1–4**
    - Why was Paul upset about the circumcision of new Christians?
    - How—and from what—has Christ made us free?
    - What does Paul mean by "fallen from grace"?
    - What are the lessons in this Biblical passage for believers today?

3. **Read 2 Corinthians 13:5; Romans 8:9**
    - What do you think of Paul's test to determine whether a person is in the faith?
    - Can it be applied to all believers?
    - What could you say to someone who thinks they fail the test?

4. **Read 1 Corinthians 1:30–31**
    - What is the significance of having Christ as our righteousness, our holiness, and our redemption?
    - Can believers experience these spiritual truths in this world?

5. **Read Galatians 6:14**
    - What does it mean to "boast in the cross of Christ"?
    - How is the world crucified to us, and us to the world, through the cross?

6. **Read Ephesians 1:3**
    - There is an old saying that a child born to a wealthy and powerful father is born with a silver spoon in his or her mouth. In what way are we, as children of our heavenly Father, born with a silver spoon in our mouth?
    - How does our God and Father give us more than any earthly father could ever give us?
    - What are some of the spiritual blessings Paul refers to in this verse?
    - Did Jesus experience these blessings of the spiritual realm?
    - Can a Christian believer experience such blessings today, in this life?

- It was God's power that raised Jesus from the dead and rolled the stone away from his tomb. He did that so people could look in and see evidence that resurrected life had come to mankind. Have you seen and experienced the evidence of Christ's resurrection in your heart?

ASK THE APOSTLE

- How is it that believers have Christ's power for victorious living?
- Discuss as a group, and then read aloud Paul's answer from Colossians 2:9–10.
- How do you personally tap into that power?

Chapter Five
Defeat Sin, Self, and Satan

Chapter Introduction

Key Bible Verses

Luke 11:15, 18; 1 John 3:8; 5:19; John 8:44; 14:30; Hebrews 9:24–26; Matthew 4:3; Genesis 3:1–13, 17–19; Revelation 12:9–10

- Is Satan real or a made-up 'super power' character that exemplifies our sinful self?
- Which is the most difficult for you to overcome: Satan or self?
- Does Satan ever give up?
- Does self ever give up?

Christ the Key

1. **Read Ephesians 6:12; Colossians 2:15; 1 John 3:8; Hebrews 2:14–15**
   - What is the nature of our battles as Christians?
   - Compare Satan (his nature, army, and power) with Jesus Christ (his nature, army, and power).
   - Satan is fighting a battle he has already lost. Where and how did Satan lose that battle?
   - Why is it important for Christians to know this fact?

2. **Read 2 Corinthians 11:14; 12:7**
   - Satan still persists in deception and torment, buffeting believers and filling their minds with false messages about themselves and their God. Can you give any examples of this kind of attack from Satan or his demons?
   - How do you respond to these assaults?
   - How did Jesus respond to Satan's attacks? Luke 4:8; Matthew 16:23

3. **Read Ephesians 2:11-18**
   - Why has the law been annulled or put out of use as a means to achieve righteousness and enter into the presence of God? Hebrews 7:18–19; 8:13; 9:24–26; Luke 16:16
   - Does this mean that as a believer you can do whatever you want? Romans 3:8; 6:1–2, 15–16; 1 Corinthians 6:12; 9:19–21; James 1:21–25; 2:12–13; Matthew 5:17–19
   - How did God disarm the spiritual principalities and powers? Colossians 2:13–15
   - How does this truth affect you as a believer?

4. **Read Colossians 2:20–23**
   - What arguments does Paul raise against following the teachings of the world when combating the flesh or sinful nature?
   - Do you agree with Paul?
   - Have you tried any of these worldly approaches? If so, how did that work out for you?

5. **Read Colossians 1:13; Ephesians 5:8–10**
   - What have Christians been delivered from?
   - As a result of this deliverance, what is expected of believers?

6. **Read 2 Corinthians 6:4–7; 10:3–4**
   - How would you describe Paul's trials?
   - What were his weapons to deal with sin, Satan, and the world?
   - Could these weapons work for believers today?

7. **Read Colossians 2:8; 2 Corinthians 11:3; 1 Corinthians 2:1–2**
   - Why do you suppose Paul keeps coming back to Christ? Galatians 2:20
   - What can we learn from Paul's experience to help us in our own walk with the Lord?

8. **Read Romans 1:16–17**
   - What did Paul mean when he said the gospel of Christ is the power of God unto salvation?
   - What role does faith have in accessing this power?

NOTES

NOTES

- How could the gospel bring Paul through all the trials and tribulations he endured?
- Is it reasonable to think this same gospel could do as much for you?

9. **Read Galatians 5:17**
   - According to this verse, what is a recurring conflict for Christians?
   - What does Paul present as the solution? Galatians 5:16, 25

ASK THE APOSTLE

♦ What is the Christian's weapon of supreme power in the battle with sin, self, and Satan?

♦ Discuss as a group, and then read aloud Paul's answer from Romans 8:10, 13.

♦ Why do believers keep trying to fight a spiritual battle in their human strength?

Spiritual Weapons

1. **Read Ephesians 5:9; Galatians 5:22–23**
   - Can we produce any of this kind of fruit in our own strength?
   - If we do manage to produce this fruit, is it the same as the fruit of the Spirit? Romans 14:23

2. **Read 1 Timothy 1:8–11**
   - What did Paul mean when he said, "The law is not given for the righteous but for the lawless and unruly"?

3. **Read Ezekiel 36:27; Romans 7:6**
   - If God's Spirit in us moves us to walk in his statutes or laws, what is our role or responsibility?

- How can we walk in God's laws and yet serve in the newness of the Spirit? Romans 8:4; Galatians 5:18
- What part do we play to live in the newness of life Christ bought for us? Romans 6:4, 11–12

4. **Read Romans 8:5–6; John 10:10**
   - Where are the two different places we can direct our attention?
   - What happens to those who seek to fulfill the desires of the flesh?
   - Where does the Bible tell us to set our minds to experience life and peace?
   - Can we engage in evil or demonic activities and associate with Jesus Christ at the same time? 1 Corinthians 10:21
   - The Greek word for life in the verses above is Zoë, the supernatural life of God given to those who accept the gospel. Do these verses suggest a believer can experience this life continually?

5. **Read Romans 13:14; John 15:5**
   - Are these two verses saying the same thing?
   - Jesus originally told his disciples to "follow me." Later he told them to "abide in me." What is the key difference in these two commands of our Lord for believers today?
   - How do Christians abide in Jesus? John 6:56, 63; Galatians 3:27

6. **Read Colossians 2:6–7; Ephesians 5:18**
   - Is this pattern a way to serve God in the newness of the Spirit?
   - What may be the easiest way to achieve this? Acts 4:31; 13:52
   - How did you receive salvation through Jesus Christ? Mark 1:15; Acts 2:38–39

7. **Read Ephesians 4:30–32; 1 Thessalonians 5:19**
   - If the only way we can live a life pleasing to God is by the Holy Spirit, how important is it to avoid grieving God's Spirit in us?
   - What are some of the ways we grieve the Spirit?
   - What are some ways we can avoid grieving the Spirit?

NOTES

- Walking in the Spirit means choosing Christ and his kingdom over Satan and his kingdom. It involves embracing the will of God, choosing his choices, and then obeying them through his power. How can our choices either impede or release supernatural power within us? John 8:29; Matthew 4:10–12; Luke 22:41–43

8. **Read James 3:2, 8; Luke 6:45**
    - What does it mean to control your tongue?
    - Try controlling your tongue for a period of time. How successful were you?
    - What are the differences between behaving (controlling the body) and becoming (a transformed heart)?
    - Which is law and which is grace?
    - Which is going to best serve Christians, and why?

9. **Read 1 Thessalonians 5:8–10**
    - How can Paul's advice help to renew our minds and increase our self-control?
    - We can collaborate with our old self and let Satan have the power in our lives, or we can cooperate with the Holy Spirit and allow Jesus Christ to have the power in our lives. Is this a one-time choice or a lifetime of choices?
    - What rewards does God offer to those who choose him over Satan and self?

ASK THE APOSTLE

- What would you say is our bottom-line strategy in defeating sin, self, and Satan?
- Discuss as a group, and then read aloud Paul's answer from Ephesians 4:22–24.
- Is overcoming sin more a matter of behaving or of becoming?

A Gospel Mind

1. **Read Ephesians 6:10–13**
   - Where would you land on a scale of 1 to 10, rating your strength in the Lord?
   - Do you think putting on the armor of God could boost your score?
   - How would you rank the power of Satan and his evil hosts on a scale of 1 to 10?
   - Why did Paul repeat his admonition to put on the complete set of armor that God supplies?

2. **Read Ephesians 6:14–17**
   - Discuss both the nature and the power of the following in our battle with evil:
     - The belt of truth. John 8:31–32
     - The breastplate of righteousness. Romans 5:17
     - The gospel of peace with God. Romans 5:1; Colossians 3:15
     - The shield of faith. Colossians 1:13–14
     - The helmet of salvation. Ephesians 1:13; 2 Corinthians 1:22
     - The sword of the Spirit, which is the word of God. Hebrews 4:12
   - If you consider the sword of the Spirit as a weapon of offence rather than one of defense, how could it be used against Satan and his demons?
   - How does the armor of God all come back to the gospel of Jesus Christ? 1 Peter 1:5; Romans 1:16; 1 Thessalonians 2:13
   - What other weapons or armor has God given us to help us choose Christ and his kingdom over Satan and the things of this world?

3. **Read 2 Corinthians 4:18; Philippians 4:8**
   - What do you think of Paul's advice to dwell on whatever things are true, honorable, righteous, pure, admirable, and noble—as well as anything of virtue or worthy of praise?
   - Could aspects of the gospel message be listed under these categories?

NOTES

- What are some other things our thoughts could dwell on that fit under Paul's categories?
- What does Paul say will happen if you put into practice what you learned and received from him? Philippians 4:9

4. **Read Romans 12:2; Ephesians 4:23**
   - What did Paul mean by "renewing your mind"?
   - How can that transform you?
   - If it is true that thought often precedes action, where does the Christian's battle take place?
   - How can this knowledge and Paul's advice help you defeat sin, self, and Satan?

5. **Read Colossians 3:2–4**
   - Why did Paul say we should set our minds on things above, on heavenly things, and on things to come? Romans 8:18, 23–25; 2 Corinthians 5:7; Titus 1:2; 2:13
   - What are some of the ways Christians can do this?

6. **Read Ephesians 3:14–21**
   - Do you think Paul's prayer for believers can be fulfilled in this life?
   - God refers to us in Scripture as his children. Do we ever fully 'grow up' spiritually?

ASK THE APOSTLE

♦ What is one thing a believer can do to focus on the journey to heaven and eternal life?

♦ Discuss as a group, and then read aloud Paul's answer from Philippians 3:13–14.

♦ How could you apply Paul's approach to your own life?

Chapter Six
The Prize—Eternal Life

Chapter Introduction

Key Bible Verses

Acts 17:16–18, 32; Colossians 1:26–27; Luke 10:21–24; John 6:39–40; 1 John 2:25; 5:11–13; Jude 1:20–21

- What are some of the quests for eternal life that you have read or heard about?

- Do you think eternal life is something people think about a lot or very rarely?

- What do you understand eternal life to be?

A Prophet Speaks

1. **Read Acts 13:28–31**
   - How solid is the evidence that Jesus rose from the dead? 1 Corinthians 15:3–7
   - What would it mean for believers if Christ has not risen? 1 Corinthians 15:12–19

2. **Read Acts 13:40–41**
   - What is a prophet of God?
   - Do we have prophets today, or is it only an Old Testament phenomenon?

3. **Read Acts 13:44–45, 49–50**
   - How did a lot of people react to the news of the resurrection of Christ in Paul's time?
   - How do a lot of people react to this news today?
   - Why do you suppose people do not believe, and some even become angry, when they are told that Jesus rose from the dead?

NOTES

- It is often said that the gospel is a good news/bad news proclamation. What is the good news? What is the bad news?
- When explaining the gospel message, is it a good idea to downplay its negative aspects?
- Did Paul think it was a good idea to minimize the truth about eternal judgment?

ASK THE APOSTLE

- Why is there less tolerance today in the church and society for the hard truths of God?
- Discuss as a group, and then read aloud Paul's answer from 2 Timothy 4:3–4.
- What is our responsibility as Christians when it comes to sharing the gospel?

Christ's Return

1. **Read 2 Timothy 2:8**
    - Why does Paul insist that Christians always remember the resurrection of the man, Jesus of Nazareth? Romans 6:9
    - Everyone will have a last day on earth. How will Christ's resurrection affect your last day? 2 Corinthians 4:14; 1 Corinthians 15:22–23; Romans 6:23

2. **Read Isaiah 65:17–18; Romans 8:19–22**
    - Why does the prophet Isaiah speak of the new Jerusalem as a jubilation and its people a joy? Revelation 21:1–4, 9–11; 22:1–5
    - What does the new creation of heaven and earth have in common with the children of God?

3. **Read 2 Thessalonians 1:6–10**
   - What are the different end states for those who do—and those who do not—accept the gospel?
   - How does this fact affect your gospel communications with family, friends, and others? Acts 4:20

4. **Read 1 Corinthians 1:18–20**
   - Why is the gospel foolishness to those who are perishing? Isaiah 29:14
   - How is the gospel the power of God to those who are being saved? Romans 1:16–17

5. **Read 1 Corinthians 1:21–25**
   - What are some of the differences between the wisdom of God and the wisdom of the world?
   - Is great intelligence, giftedness, or education necessary to understand the gospel?
   - What is necessary to understand and accept the gospel? Mark 10:15; Jeremiah 29:13

6. **Read 1 Corinthians 2:6–7; 15:42–43**
   - Do people really believe that God will share his divine, eternal glory with us?
   - Do you believe this? 2 Thessalonians 1:10; 2:13–14; Philippians 3:20–21
   - Can you join Paul in rejoicing in the hope of sharing the glory of God? Romans 5:1–2
   - Can you also join Paul in rejoicing in trials and tribulations? Romans 5:3–4

NOTES

ASK THE APOSTLE

- Why is it good for Christians to long for the return of Jesus?
- Discuss as a group, and then read aloud Paul's answer from 2 Timothy 4:8.
- Are you eagerly looking forward to Christ's appearance? Why?

Our New Body

1. **Read 1 Corinthians 15:44–49**
   - What are the differences between our earthly body and our resurrected spiritual body?
   - What strikes you as the most significant aspect of the new spiritual body?

2. **Read Romans 8:10–11; Colossians 3:3–4**
   - Try to arrange all these words into one sentence: Christ. Spirit. God. Life. Believer. Glory.

3. **Read Matthew 24:29–31; 1 Thessalonians 4:16–17**
   - In Genesis we read that God commanded light into existence: "Let there be light!" The first day. How potent is God's Word?
   - In 1 Thessalonians we read that at the last day, the Lord will descend with another command. What will happen then?

4. **Read Ephesians 1:15–18**
   - Why would Paul pray that new believers would know the surpassing riches of the glory of God's inheritance for the saints? Romans 15:13; 1 Peter 1:3–9

5. **Read 1 Corinthians 15:58**
   - Why does Paul insist that we stand firm in the hope of immortality and always be abounding in the Lord's work?
   - How are these two activities or behaviors connected? 1 Thessalonians 1:3
   - How do we know our labor in the Lord is not in vain? 2 Corinthians 4:17; Colossians 3:23–24

6. **Read Philippians 3:17–19**
   - Why does Paul give this tearful, yet stern, warning?
   - When Paul speaks of those who are living as enemies of the cross of Christ, is he talking about Christians or unbelievers?
   - How can Christians benefit from Paul's admonition?

7. **Read Philippians 3:20–21**
   - As Christians, where is our citizenship?
   - What are the benefits of this citizenship?
   - What does this mean for our life and time in this world? Hebrews 11:13–16
   - Is eternal life a gift or a choice—or both?

NOTES

═══════════ **ASK THE APOSTLE** ═══════════

- What will happen to the Christians who are still alive when Jesus returns?
- Discuss as a group, and then read aloud Paul's answer from 1 Corinthians 15:50–53.
- What kind of feelings does Paul's statement stir up in you?

NOTES

Chapter Seven
God's Plan for You

Chapter Introduction

Key Bible Verses

Jeremiah 29:11; Romans 8:19–22; 2 Peter 3:10–13; Revelation 22:3–5; John 10:10; Acts 1:8–9; 10:44–45; 15:7–9; 2 Corinthians 3:18; 1 Corinthians 15:53

- How is God's perspective different from our human perspective concerning plans for the future?
- God has plans for our lives—both an eternal plan and a plan for us here on earth. How much is God aware of our lives here?
- How does God stay connected with people?

God's Grand Plan

1. **Read Romans 4:17; 8:30; 1 Corinthians 6:2–3**
   - Compare God's statements to Abraham with God's statements concerning Christians.
   - How are they alike?
   - How are they different?

2. **Read Romans 4:18–21**
   - What did Abraham realize with respect to fulfilling God's plan?
   - Praise is the highest expression of faith. Do you agree with that statement?
   - Abraham, in the absence of physical evidence or hope, chose to trust in God. Can you think of a time you trusted in God even when there seemed to be no reason to have hope?
   - What must we focus on in times of doubt or uncertainty to avoid becoming double-minded about our faith?

3. **Read Hebrews 11:11–12**
   - How was Sarah able to fulfill God's plan for her?
   - What was the end result of the faith of Abraham and Sarah concerning God's promise?
   - What could we learn from Abraham and Sarah to help us in our Christian walk?

4. **Read 1 Corinthians 6:11**
   - Is it possible to be washed of our sins, made holy, and pronounced righteous and yet not feel any of these things?
   - An old Christian adage is that feeling follows faith. Is this true?
   - Why is it important for Christians to have complete faith in God and his promises?

5. **Read 2 Thessalonians 2:13–14**
   - How are these Bible verses similar to God's plan for Abraham and Sarah to have a son?
   - How can believers be absolutely certain of the fulfillment of this promise?
   - What are some other to-be-fulfilled promises of God concerning Christians? 1 Corinthians 6:2–3; Revelation 3:21; 22:3–5
   - Do you trust God to fulfill these promises?

6. **Read 2 Corinthians 6:17–7:1**
   - Why is this command of God a key part of his plan for every believer? 2 Timothy 1:9; Ephesians 2:10; Titus 2:14; 1 Thessalonians 4:3, 7
   - Why would Paul say that, having God's promises, we should seek to be holy? Genesis 18:17–19; Hebrews 12:14
   - Do you believe God chose you for salvation?
   - How do you know that? Ephesians 1:4; Colossians 3:12; Matthew 22:14; John 6:26–29, 37, 44, 65; Acts 13:48; 16:14
   - If Abraham and Sarah could have a baby even though they were physically incapable, could it be possible for Christians to live a holy life even though—in their own strength—they are incapable?

NOTES

ASK THE APOSTLE

- How is Abraham the father of all who believe?

- Discuss as a group, and then read aloud Paul's answer from Galatians 3:6–9.

- How did Scripture announce the gospel beforehand?

Fulfilling God's Plan

1. **Read 1 Timothy 1:3–5**
   - How does the gospel give believers this kind of love? Romans 5:5

   - If you do not have a clean conscience, then you do not understand the gospel. Is that an accurate statement? Why or why not? 1 Peter 1:22; Hebrews 10:2, 10, 14

   - Do you think people can love perfectly without a saving faith in Jesus Christ?

   - Why did Jesus say that people will recognize believers by their love for one another? John 13:35

2. **Read Colossians 1:4–6**
   - How does faith in Christ and the hope of eternal life contribute to our love for other believers?

   - According to the apostle Paul, what one command of Jesus fulfills the entire law? Mark 12:31; Romans 13:8–10

   - What is the nature of the love Jesus and Paul were talking about? Romans 5:5; Galatians 5:22

   - How can Christians demonstrate that kind of love? 1 Corinthians 13:4–7; Romans 12:9–10; Colossians 3:13; Galatians 3:5; Ephesians 4:1–3; Matthew 18:21–22

   - Why would Jesus say that the one who loves little has been forgiven little? Luke 7:47

- What is the relationship between forgiveness and love? Ephesians 4:32–5:2

3. **Read Philippians 2:13**
   - Why does God give believers both the desire and the power to fulfill his plans for us?
   - God had a plan for Sarah and Abraham's life, and he intervened in their lives to make it happen. How does God intervene in a Christian's life to fulfill his plans?

4. **Read Philippians 2:14–16**
   - How and why would Paul expect believers to do everything without grumbling or arguing?
   - What does Paul mean by "shine as lights in the world"?
   - How can you participate in fulfilling God's plans for you?

5. **Read Galatians 3:1–3**
   - What role or responsibility does the flesh have in fulfilling God's plans for believers?
   - What is the role of the Holy Spirit in fulfilling those same plans? Galatians 3:5; Romans 14:17

NOTES

ASK THE APOSTLE

- Believers work hard to get along, so why do they end up arguing?
- Discuss as a group, and then read aloud Paul's answer from 1 Corinthians 3:3.
- If this is the case for you, what are some new things you could try?

The Holiness Path

1. **Read Romans 6:17–18**
   - What transforming teachings of Paul are referred to here?
   - What is the change it made in people?
   - Can we expect the same change in people today?

2. **Read Romans 6:19–23**
   - To whom and to what do people normally present themselves for service?
   - What is the end of that path?
   - Why should believers present themselves to the service of righteousness?
   - What is the end of that path?

3. **Read Romans 6:11–13; 12:1**
   - Paul says to present ourselves holy and acceptable to God as instruments of righteousness. Why can believers actually do that? Colossians 1:21–23
   - What does Paul mean by offering ourselves to God "as alive from the dead"? Ephesians 2:1–7
   - Why do people resist presenting themselves completely to God and to his service?
   - What could you do to help someone overcome that resistance?
   - How could you work toward overcoming that same resistance in yourself?

4. **Read 1 Corinthians 15:1–2**
   - Why does Paul keep telling believers to hold fast to the gospel and to stand firm in the faith? 1 Corinthians 16:13; Galatians 5:1; 2 Thessalonians 2:15
   - Paul said there is a truth that leads to godliness or piety. What is it? Titus 1:1–2

5. **Read Luke 18:8**
   - Why will Jesus be looking for faith when he returns?

- What do believers need to be doing as they wait for the return of Christ? 1 Timothy 6:12; Philippians 3:12; 1 Peter 1:13–15; 2 Peter 3:10–12; Jude 20–21
- How much can we do by ourselves to please God? John 15:5
- How much can we do to please God through Christ by the Holy Spirit? Philippians 4:13

6. **Read Philippians 2:12–13**
   - If God is both prompting us and empowering us to do his will, what is our role in 'working out' our salvation?
   - Why did Paul continually exhort and encourage believers, praying that God would make them worthy of his calling? 2 Thessalonians 1:11; Colossians 1:9–12; 1 Thessalonians 2:12

7. **Read Psalm 37:5–6; 1 Thessalonians 5:23–24**
   - When people are committed to a hospital, they submit themselves to doctors and nurses, trusting they will be well cared for. It is the same when we commit ourselves and our way to the Lord. We are putting ourselves into God's hands, trusting him for our care and well-being.
   - If we trust doctors and nurses, can we trust God to take care of us as we put our faith in him to do so?
   - If God promises to lovingly care for us, to bring forth our righteousness, and to present us perfect and holy at the coming of Jesus, why is it hard for people to commit their lives to God?
   - Can you commit your life to the Lord and his care? If not, what is the obstacle for you?

ASK THE APOSTLE

- How can Christians walk worthy of the calling to which they are called?
- Discuss as a group, and then read aloud Paul's answer from Ephesians 4:1–3.
- Is there anything you would like to add to this?

NOTES

Epilogue
Famous Last Words

Chapter Introduction

Key Bible Verses

1 Timothy 4:15–16

- What was the most helpful insight you picked up from the conversations with Paul?
- What is one thing you can begin to do to make it your own and a part of your daily life?

A Precious Jewel

1. **Read Ephesians 1:13; 2:8; Colossians 2:13; Romans 5:1–2, 17; 6:23; 8:2**
   - What are some different features and benefits of the gospel that believers have in Jesus Christ?
   - Which facet of the gospel appeals most to you? Why is that?

2. **Read 2 Timothy 2:8–10**
   - Why did Paul say he had suffered for the gospel?
   - Did Paul have other incentives to preach the gospel? 1 Corinthians 9:16–17; 2 Corinthians 5:14
   - What is your motivation to share the good news with others?
   - Paul said the gospel of God is not restrained. What did he mean by that, and why is it so?
   - It has been said that the gospel is the work of grace in our hearts. What does that mean?
   - Why did Paul keep referring to the gospel as "the word of truth"? 2 Corinthians 6:7; Ephesians 1:13; 2 Timothy 2:15

3. **Read Matthew 24:9–10, 12–13; 2 Timothy 2:12**
   - Why did Jesus forewarn his disciples in this way?

- Was the apostle Paul saying basically the same thing?
- What can believers today take from these teachings?
- Do a word search of the New Testament for the word "endure." What does Christian endurance look like?

4. **Read Romans 2:3–11**
   - What is reserved for those who do not obey Jesus Christ and the gospel? 2 Thessalonians 1:7–9; 2:9–12
   - What is reserved for those who do receive Christ and his gospel? John 3:15; 6:54; 10:27–28; Romans 6:23; Titus 3:7; 1 John 2:25; 5:11, 13; Jude 1:21
   - Why do the Biblical warnings concerning those who refuse to respond to the gospel often frighten or anger people?
   - How will these facts influence your personal ministry to others regarding the gospel?

5. **Read Galatians 6:7–9**
   - How are these verses declarations of both judgment and encouragement?
   - When will those who persist in doing good reap what they have sown?

ASK THE APOSTLE

- If our salvation is certain, why must we endure to the end?
- Discuss as a group, and then read aloud Paul's answer from 1 Corinthians 9:24–27.
- Is there a kind of tension between 'God does it' and 'we do it'?

God's Amazing Grace

1. **Read 2 Timothy 2:1**
   - How are believers strengthened by the grace that is in Jesus Christ and the gospel?
   - Discuss how the word "grace" captures the essence of the gospel message with respect to:
     - The nature of God. Ephesians 2:7; Galatians 1:15; Ephesians 2:8; 2 Thessalonians 1:12; 2:16; Hebrews 2:9
     - The work of Jesus on the cross. Titus 2:11; Ephesians 1:6; 2 Corinthians 12:9; Titus 2:12–13
     - The Holy Spirit in us. 1 Corinthians 15:10; Romans 1:16; 2 Corinthians 1:12; 9:8; Colossians 1:5–6; Acts 20:32
   - What did Jesus mean when he said his grace is sufficient? 2 Corinthians 12:9
   - When you think of God's grace, what do you think of? Forgiveness? Peace? The gospel?
   - Why do all of Paul's letters to the churches he established begin (and many close) with the words "grace to you"?
   - Do a word search to see what other writers of the New Testament said about the grace of God.
   - Is it possible to live and walk in the grace of God every hour? Every minute? Acts 11:23; 13:43
   - Why do you suppose the last verse in the Bible consists of a prayer that the grace of the Lord Jesus Christ be with all the saints? Revelation 22:21 (Majority Text)

2. **Read Galatians 1:6–9**
   - Why was Paul so upset with the Galatian believers?
   - Is there another, better gospel than this one of the grace of God in Jesus Christ? Romans 5:17; Acts 20:32; Hebrews 13:9

ASK THE APOSTLE

- What is the best way to tell others the good news of God's incredible grace?
- Discuss as a group, and then read aloud Paul's answer from Colossians 4:5–7.
- How does the Holy Spirit help us follow Paul's advice?

Paul's Final Advice

1. **Read 1 Thessalonians 5:16–22**
   - How does the gospel contribute to a believer's ability to obey each of the seven brief directives in these verses?

2. **Read Romans 12:12**
   - Rejoice. Endure. Pray. Do you have a favorite Bible verse for one of these commands?
   - Why do these three directives come up so frequently in the New Testament?
   - Which is the easiest for you to do?
   - Which is the hardest?

3. **Read Philippians 4:4**
   - The Greek word often translated as "always" means literally "at all times." The command to rejoice in the Lord (in his grace, Spirit, forgiveness, eternal life, and hope of glory) calls for a constant, habitual action. Can a believer rejoice in the Lord at all times, regardless of circumstances? 1 Peter 1:3–9

4. **Read Philippians 4:6–7**
   - Why does Paul place so much emphasis on prayer?
   - Discuss Paul's instructions regarding:
     - Constant, unrelenting prayer. Romans 12:12
     - Being vigilant in prayer with thanksgiving. Colossians 4:2
     - Praying always in the Spirit. Ephesians 6:18
   - What could believers do to strengthen their prayer lives?

- What is the role of the Holy Spirit in effective prayer? Romans 8:26

5. **Read 2 Timothy 4:7–8; Philippians 3:17**
    - How and why was Paul's service to the Lord to be rewarded?
    - Paul lived the kind of life he encouraged other believers to live. How do you think that affected Paul's confidence about the reward he would have in heaven?
    - Why is it essential that the gospel teachings of Paul move from our head down to our heart? Colossians 3:16
    - What can we do to help this process in our own life?

6. **Read Colossians 1:4–6; Romans 6:17–18**
    - The Bible records that those who heard the gospel and came under the teachings of Paul were transformed. In what ways have you been changed by the gospel?
    - What can Christians do today that others may come under—and obey from the heart—the teachings of the apostle Paul and the Bible?

ASK THE APOSTLE

- What should we do if a believer is caught in a transgression?
- Discuss as a group, and then read aloud Paul's answer from Galatians 6:1.
- Is there any room for judgment in Paul's instructions?

NOTES